A PRIVATE BANKING SYSTEM FOR CANADIANS

ALBERTO STORELLI

Gurpal (Paul) Sidhu
Ph No. 403-613-8700
Email: gsidhu683nnc@wfgmail.ca
http://www.wfgconnects.com/paulsidhu

ISBN: 0993850804
ISBN 13: 9780993850806

DEDICATION

This book is dedicated to my wife Demi and my beautiful children Nico and Melina. You are my light...your patience with my passions means so much to me.

Gurpal (Paul) Sidhu
Ph No. 403-613-8700
Email: gsidhu683nnc@wfgmail.ca
http://www.wfgconnects.com/paulsidhu

ACKNOWLEDGEMENTS

Demetra Storelli	Editor
Dina Milani	Editor
Chris Redcliffe	Associate Editor
Noelle Nikas	Cover Design
John Perre	First IBC Mentor
Giovanni Bitelli	Insurance Mentor
Pino Storelli	Original Mentor

I would like to thank my father, Pino Storelli, for being my first mentor in the financial planning industry. You always knew dividend paying life insurance was the best place to store savings. I would also like to thank Harp Purewall for introducing me to the Bank on Yourself system which led me to discovering that there is a better way.

TABLE OF CONTENTS

From "*The Prescriptions for Wealth*"- Dr. Tom McVie:

THE PROCESS

CHAPTER FOUR

***"The best mind-altering drug is truth."* – Lily Tomlin**

What if you knew about a place where you could store your money, earn a guaranteed yield on it and still be able to use your money at the same time... without any penalties...no loss of interest, no fees and no service charge?

What if you knew that you could use your money to make it grow more money and that when your money grew it wouldn't face any further taxes on the growth?

What if you could continue to use the growth of your money and by using it the only down side would be that you'd have more money to use?

What if you could do all this and still have no debt? No creditors? No liabilities?

What if you were told this secure and safe place to grow your money has been around for over 200 years and that it is used by thousands of people, business owners, corporations and bankers daily?

What if it were known to you that the process to accomplish all this was very simple and easy to access?

What emotions would you experience realizing that nobody has ever taken the time to tell you about this?

What else would you want to know about this process?

INTRODUCTION

"Someone is in the shade today because someone planted a tree a long time ago"
–Warren Buffet

The problem had become painfully clear. What I didn't expect to realize in the process of discovering Infinite Banking was that I was part of the problem! The problem was special interest and fragmentation that had engulfed the financial planning industry. The financial planning textbooks had been leaving out guaranteed solutions that were extremely effective. I had suspected this for a long time, however, could not provide the guaranteed solution beyond what was readily accepted in the mainstream.

In the summer of 2011, I became aware of an "alternative" way of managing one's finances. I pride myself in being an open minded reader and life long learner. How had I not heard of this low risk way to get ahead? I spend an average of two hours a day reading industry research, current events and books of all types and genres--how did I miss this? I am not the only one! 99.9 % of registered financial advisors/financial planners, like me, could not explain what is going to be explained in this book. They know parts of what will be explained, like I did, however, not the whole story. Not even close. I admittedly, was in this camp as well.

I had what Mr. Nelson Nash, the Pioneer of a concept called Infinite Banking, calls "The Arrival Syndrome". In Nash's words:"This phenomenon probably limited the achievements of mankind more than anything else. When this "thing" infects us, we stop growing, stop learning. We ROT! We turn off or tune out the ability to receive inspiration – because we already know all there is to know.

Every day I encounter one or many who have this illness. I had it and fought through it but realize that it's something I need to fight daily to prevent from coming back. Unfortunately, the more "educated" we are, the more this syndrome infects us. Or paradoxically, the people with the least education, like to tell us how things are. We all have relatives like this. Sadly, I can lump the majority of humanity in this camp.

Every day is a struggle to not let this illness infect my conversations and prejudices. It is a tough task! It is a must, however, if one wants the most out of life!

One of my favourite stories that highlights this illness is attributed to Socrates. Socrates stated, "The only true wisdom is in knowing you know nothing." I use a variation of this famous phrase daily.

Alvin Toffler, the author of "*Future Shock*", is credited with highlighting a reality that can't be ignored in this day in age. " the illiterate of the 21st century will not be those who cannot read and write, but those who cannot learn, unlearn and relearn." The words of this writer and futurist will ring more and more true as the exponential age we live in today turns our world on its head. This undeniable truth will be for the better of most people however; for those that choose not to rid themselves of the "Arrival Syndrome" will wonder why they got run over by this wave of exponential change and awareness for humanity.

This is the challenge. Never stop learning. It took me over ten months to deprogram myself and realize there is a better way to compliment, and in some circumstances, replace entirely the contemporary way of creating financial independence. I typically advocate a balanced and diversified approach. This book will highlight how and why the Infinite Banking system can be integrated into the quest for financial independence for individuals and corporations of all sophistications. Beginners, or the very financially sophisticated and astute can create better results without taking risks, using the most simple principles of private banking. This system is known as the "Infinite Banking Concept" or "Bank on Yourself".

Chapter 1

LIES AGREED UPON

"All truths experience 3 stages. They are first ridiculed, then violently opposed and only much later, are accepted as self evident"
– Schopenhauer

In the fall of 2008, I slept an average of three hours a night. Anyone in my industry who didn't have severe sleep deprivation, likely, did not care about their clients' well-being. The scenario we did not ever wish to see or deluded ourselves to be a relic of the past, was happening more fiercely than had even occurred in the Great Depression. The Great Depression caused the US markets to go down 90% over three years. It took two decades to recoup those highs. This is never brought up in the financial planning textbooks. The stock market did not go down 90% in 2008/2009. It felt like it did. It went down approximately 50%.

Markets were moving down and up five to ten percent a day! I had diversified my clients into other, non-correlated asset classes. However, this violent volatility had surpassed the violence and volatility of the Great Depression and were less severe re-enactments, every other day, it seemed, of the 1987 crash that brought down the financial markets 25% in one day. This is not what anyone had signed up for; investors or financial professionals alike. Lehman brothers had been allowed to fail. This shocked everyone in the industry as many smaller companies had been bailed out. Much larger ones such as AIG had also been bailed out in a way that did not create massive contagion. Conceptually I am not a fan of bailing out any corporate entity of any kind. The moral hazards are endless. The financial system had been allowed to exist with many zombie entities that sadly, were too big to fail. The Federal Reserve, for better or worse, was a lender of last resort that was supposed to contain the contagion of a massive failure of a financial entity as large as the Lehman Brothers. This did not happen. A two trillion dollar margin call ensued and the Libor rate (the overnight rate banks lend to each other at) went from around one percent to over five percent in a matter of days. A global credit freeze ensued and we had what has been dubbed 'The Great Recession'. Many parties are to blame; government, bankers, Wall Street and amateur investors/homeowner who naively believed real estate only goes up. A failure of government is at the root of all of this.

I will shed some light on that theme throughout this book. I am not cheerleading Wall Street whatsoever here but I am disgusted with the exclusive blame shouldered on Wall Street. Napoleon Bonaparte is credited with the phrase "history is a set of lies agreed upon". The history that will be written will undoubtedly read that bankers and Wall Street greed brought the economy to the brink of the abyss. The reality is that the sub prime crises was multiple decades in the making thanks to governments colluding with Wall Street and wishing to see home ownership north of 70%.

I am very sympathetic to high home ownership rates and think owning a home is an admirable wish. Reality tells me that the unintended consequences of high ownership rates are shouldered by an unsuspecting group. That group is always the taxpayer. The sub prime crises did not need to be as extreme as it was.

Leadership at the Federal Reserve allowed the alumni at Goldman Sachs to make one of their biggest competitors disappear – Lehman Brothers. Who would have been competing for all of the government bond underwriting head to head with Goldman? Lehman Brothers, as their bond desks were comparable in size. Oliver Stone made a movie about it and changed the names to avoid legal slander charges. I'm going to call it for what it is: crony capitalism at its worst. This had little to do with free markets. It was central planning gone bad with crony friends of government profiting stupendously.

The bailouts did not work as the stock market went down another 40% the following four months after these bailouts became law. They worked if you were an executive that gave politicians contributions, which resulted in you obtaining a large executive bonus not too long after the financial carnage. The early March 2009 whispers of reversing mark-to-market accounting rules, are what caused the market to whipsaw northward. The rules were finally relaxed the week of April 2nd, 2009. Now banks did not have to raise money on a quarterly basis for balance sheets collateralized by an illiquid asset: real estate. Mark-to-Market rules where the financial equivalent of pouring gasoline on a fire. US Banks had to have extra capital on hand based on the decreasing value of their real estate on a quarterly basis. This was the silent assassin known as mark-to-market accounting. Mark-to-market is what caused titan banking outfits like Wachovia, Washington Mutual, Bear Stearns, Lehman Brothers and countless others to become insolvent literally overnight. They couldn't raise capital fast enough to deal with an accounting rule that was added to allow banks to expand THEIR balance sheets. So let's get banks to value their illiquid real estate holdings quarterly so they can engage in more real estate madness and lend even more money as the increasing real estate holdings value would allow them to lend more as the collateral never goes down right? Mark-to-Market was created to enable a mechanism to quickly and efficiently expand real estate lending as loan portfolios became healthier as a result of the rising real estate collateral. The government blessed this as more homeowners equals more tax revenue and happier voters. The problem obviously is when the government tries to engineer a never before seen soft landing in the economic cycle.

When real estate values fall, the reversal of real estate balance sheet values creates an insolvency problem like none other seen since the Great Depression. Mark-to-market works in reverse when markets go sour. Many factors came together to cause the great recession.

I have simply highlighted the greatest failures of government here in unison with irresponsible lending and borrowing and Wall Street collusion.

The reason I go through this painful history is simple. We are taught in our financial planning textbooks that portfolio construction will save us from these extreme ills. The failures of government and the financial community will happen again. Likely, just after we have forgotten what recently happened. When trouble arises, the correlation of your stock market holdings, no matter how cleverly engineered are close to or virtually one. Simply, it goes in the same direction violently: down! There is an asset class that doesn't experience this type of volatility and has an over 30 year history of delivering a mimimum of seven percent after tax to the investor. This asset savings class is the guaranteed bedrock of Infinite Banking.

Investors saving for retirement are supposed to explicitly trust the Pirates of Manhattan (and the politicians in bed with them) with the majority of our savings and their investments. Faith requires the abandonment of all critical faculties. Your future should not be based on faith! It should be based on unbiased leadership and unbiased financial advice. For the majority of people, this requires portfolios that are largely composed of guaranteed income for life. I say this because, after 15 years in the financial services industry, I realize as lucidly as ever that most investors are conservative and have modest sophistication. In the absence of adversity, most people will say they understand the risks and are comfortable with volatility. Their tone quickly changes once unpredicatable situations arise. The solution for this is guaranteed income for life for all or a major portion of their portfolio from a private counterparty that has reserves to back up these guarantees. A private pension or portfolio that had guarantees like our parents' parents had. This has always been possible. The Pirates of Manhattan, along with their paid for political leaders, changed the game in a way that favoured the solutions offered exclusively by Wall Steet and the imitators of Wall Street.

The bull market of 1980 to 2000 was the longest bull market in history. *"The Great Wall Street Retirement Scam"* by Rick Bueter is a must read to understand the history of The Great Retirement Experiment known as ERISA. ERISA and its significance in giving the Pirates of Manhattan the responsibility of managing unsophisticated people's retirement planning will be explained in more detail in Chapter Five.

I was a "term and invest the difference" disciple the first twelve years of my career. It made sense to all of us. Insurance is a necessary evil, right? Not an asset class of choice. I had very little opposition from my clientele about this "obvious" reality. Reality, as life teaches, is a lot different than what is "obvious" or apparent. Just like the fact that the sun does not go around the earth, the reality about the true benefits of a dividend paying whole life insurance policy were not apparent to me even though I was taught by the office employees of one of the top three life insurance companies in Canada. I was taught the less optimal way to structure my clients' affairs. I was taught what most people know about dividend paying whole life insurance. The most important parts were left out. Not intentionally, but because no one was looking for what Nelson Nash realized was staring him in the face in the early 1980's.

The sad reality is I was part of the problem and most of my industry is still in the dark about this. I was fortunate to have a colleague, whom I brainstormed client solutions with, who insisted I learn how to "Bank on Yourself". Simply put, it is a guaranteed income for life platform that, in the first few decades of this financial plan, turns your expenses into assets. Then, whenever you wish, you turn those assets into guaranteed income for life. This income would not exist if you consumed and paid interest to banks as we have been conditioned to do since the beginning of time. Chapter Five will elaborate more on the reason, I feel, "Term Insurance and invest the difference" has been championed as much as it has been.

I was the ultimate skeptic and went through a ten month journey to prove that Pamela Yellen and Nelson Nash, two of America's experts on Infinite Banking, were wrong. After I had completed reading sixteen books on the theme, I was extremely upset. I could have completely side swiped two to 50% bear markets if I had implemented this approach comprehensively for my clientele in the last 15 years. Many of my clients' banking systems would have been completely capitalized and would have seen them well on their way to reversing the 90/10 problem my industry does not address at all. I will explain the 90/10 problem in Chapter Three-Maximizing Your Potential.

After the anger towards my well-intentioned financial trainers/mentors subsided, I realized I had almost no competition in enlightening the people I serve about this financial antidote to irresponsible finance and recurring failures of government.

Most of the Financial Planning industry is in the dark to this age old approach, precisely because the interests are aligned against the common investor. The fruits of the best business in the world: banking; are not to be taught and shared, of course. Why teach the masses to compete with the financial titans? It's not a conspiracy per se; it's just special interest going about its business as it does in all aspects of society. The industrial military complex, western medicine, religion and contemporary finance are all offspring of a multiple decade or century long lobbying efforts that will be around until the end of ages. Seeing through these lobbying realities is where true awareness resides.

This age old approach has been around for over 150 years without losses incurred by those that took this guaranteed approach. No Canadian policy owner has ever lost money in a life insurance policy from a company failure. The theme of why this approach needs to be learned by everyone has to do with the following question:

What do you think builds more wealth, increasing the rate of return of your savings and investments or decreasing the cost to build wealth? Most people answer the former. The latter is true, however, especially if you purchase your depreciables (like cars and holidays) with your own private banking system – otherwise known as the Infinite Banking System. We are taught that it is necessary to take risks to get ahead. This is an example of a lie that has been agreed upon by the special interest groups that want to oversee all of our assets. They deserve some. However, in the following chapters will demonstrate why I believe it is foolish to let them handle all of our hard earned money.

DOES THE RETIREMENT/ EDUCATION SAVINGS PLAN YOU CURRENTLY HAVE OR ARE CONSIDERING ...	RRSP	TFSA	RESP	BANK ON YOURSELF PLANS
Give you guaranteed, predictable growth?	?	?	×	✓
Lock in your principal and growth, even when the market crashes?	?	?	×	✓
Give you control of your money without Government restrictions and penalties?	×	✓	×	✓
Give you tax-free income?	×	✓	×	✓
Let you use your money in the plan without penalties, however and whenever you want?	×	✓	×	✓
Let you use your money in the plan yet still have it grow as though you didn't touch it?	×	×	×	✓
Let you access your money without liquidating your investments?	×	×	×	✓
Allow you to fund it every year, without limits imposed by the government?	×	×	×	✓
Finish funding itself if you die prematurely?	×	×	×	✓
Tell you the minimum guaranteed value of the plan on the day you expect to tap into it, and at any point along the way?	×	×	×	✓

Chapter 2

SPEND, AND GROW RICH! OPPORTUNITY COST IS A PARAMOUNT CONCEPT

"Never let formal education get in the way of your learning"
-Mark Twain

Opportunity Cost: potential gain foregone from other alternatives when one alternative is chosen.

My breakthrough in getting past my "Arrival Syndrome" that blinded me from the benefits of a private banking system came when I was simply shown how a private banking system can recapture lost interest and conservatively earn back the depreciation of everything I consume over time. The analogy that best describes what a paradigm shift this simple insight was is the story of the arrow in the FedEx logo. I have long admired FedEx the company. Fred Smith was told his business idea was useless. His iconic story as a business visionary is well chronicled. What I didn't realize was that over the last three decades of staring at FedEx signs obliviously, staring at me all the time, was the arrow. I never saw it, and it was there the whole time. Look at the logo below. Do you see the arrow? Hint, it's closer to the end of the word and it's in white. It was there the whole time. Now, when I see a FedEx truck, it's impossible for me not to see the arrow! Just like it's impossible for me not to see the foolish ways we have been acquiring all of our major and minor purchases all our lives.

Just like the arrow was there the whole time, the powerful financial strategy known as Infinite Banking was there the whole time! It was right under the whole financial services industry's nose, mine included.

It was not until the adversity of the early 1980's that Mr. Nelson Nash's need for a financial solution to his leveraged predicament, at 21% interest rates, caused him to "discover" a financial and age old solution that has been around for over 150 years; the contractual power of dividend paying life insurance. He could borrow at much more favorable terms from his life insurance policies than from his bank. Not only that, it could be used with no fuss or underwriting to purchase what one wished. If you paid yourself back like a responsible banker, you would not only not be indebted to a third party and keep the interest costs on your balance sheet, you would reverse the scourge of consumption which is depreciation. On top of reversing the financial cancer of depreciation, we can benefit from becoming the banker and receiving the interest normally paid to others. Quite simply, you are earning dividends on money residing in your Banking System. As the owner of a dividend paying life insurance policy with a mutual company, you are a mutual owner of the life insurance company and share in its profits. The natural benefit is increased wealth without risk. This is a powerful and timeless example of guaranteed income for life!

Do you remember the Freedom 55 ads of the 80's and even today? Participating whole life is what they were talking about! The original way to save with flexibility and receive better returns than term deposits has always been dividend paying life insurance. I knew that and took it for granted as being one of the solutions available to financial advisors that I have used in situations where I thought it was warranted. The insurance industry, in my opinion, had understated the comprehensive benefits that were always there in a dividend paying life insurance policy.

Many people have used the contractual benefits within a life insurance policy to borrow, purchase items, and in many cases start businesses with the available cash values in a dividend paying life insurance policy. Some of the most famous people who have done this are: Walt Disney (founded Disneyland with the cash residing in his life insurance policy), Ray Kroc (founder of McDonalds), JC Penney, and closer to home Jim Pattison all started their business' with the help of their dividend paying life insurance policy (Banking System). I have a testimonial from Mr. Jim Pattison, addressed to me, and signed by him in the living benefits chapter of this book. Mr. Nelson Nash was the first we know of who published this "discovery " to the extent that is obvious to us today, and started teaching it as a way to obtain financial independence from the financial slavery we know as interest, taxes, loss of consumption dollars and inflation. **The benefits are not theoretical, they are factual and the Opportunity Cost benefit is one the strategy's greatest strengths.**

While you are accumulating money, your money is growing. While you are using the money, your money is growing. Spend and grow rich! This sounds impossible! This is an example of when the arrival syndrome was working against me. I thought that the only ways to purchase things was with cash or credit. I was wrong. Of the two payment options, cash was the most responsible way to do this. Don't pay interest to someone. Avoid that expense altogether was a non-sophisticated approach to financial responsibility that is timeless. It obviously is the better way to go when you compare it to the other way we have been taught, the financing option that involves the lending cartel that understandably does not want competition.

This is where the power of the financial paradigm shift becomes ever clearer. When we pay cash for our purchases we destroy the capital – FOREVER. Depreciation can't be reversed. The only exceptions are savings, sound investments and collectibles you won't consume or use. No one can prove me different. Simply put: **Opportunity cost is what we could have reasonably earned on that money if we had invested it or simply saved it. This is one of the major themes of the benefits of becoming your own banker.**

As you see below, if you could get a safe and reasonable 5% rate of return, a $40,000 car cost you in "opportunity" over $106,000 over 30 years. If you can make seven percent on your cash, which could equate to over $304,490. That considerable sum of capital, which would have traditionally been "lost", can make an incredible difference in someone's standard of living during their retirement years. Paying cash may seem like a great alternative to financing, which it is compared to traditional borrowing, but is it the best way to make a purchase?

Years	5%	7%	10%	12%
5	$51,051	$56,102	$64,420	$70,493
10	$65,155	$78.686	$103,794	$124,233
20	$106,131	$154,787	$269,100	$385,851
30	$172,877	$304,490	$697,976	$1.4 Million

What if there was a better way to acquire both major and minor expenses? What if the average family earning $80,000 a year could ADD over one million dollars in the course of their lifetime with no risk, simply by changing the way they acquire their major expenses? This is why the book "Bank on Yourself" by Pamel Yellen is such a runaway best seller. I was inspired to change, unlearn and relearn this better way of acquiring things after first reading Nelson Nash's book, "Becoming Your Own Banker". I then read "Bank on Yourself" and FINALLY realized why this is for everyone. I could not sleep the night I read "Bank On Yourself". The impact this strategy can have on the population is a massive paradigm shift that I believe can have a legacy similar to the legacy the printing press had . The only exception is if you are not disciplined. The risk is your discipline as Nelson Nash explains in his grocery store example in "Becoming Your own Banker."

So coming back to the question I brought to your attention in Chapter 1: "What do you think builds more wealth? Increasing the rate of return of your savings and investments or decreasing the cost to build wealth?", You can hopefully now see that by keeping more of the money you make, you can trump the need to earn a great return that involves uncertainty and risk. If you like taking entrepreneurial risks, the Infinite Banking system will enable you to perform even better than if you paid cash traditionally for them. This is discussed in Chapter Nine-*Enable Your Investments to Perform Better with Infinite Banking Concept.*

The Infinite Banking system allows you to earn money on your capital conservatively by becoming the banker and receiving the interest normally paid to others, and by reversing depreciation on all consumption. This is all done tax-free when properly structured. The natural result is wealth without risk. This wealth, which would not exist by buying items traditionally, can be turned into a guaranteed income for life within the Infinite Banking system that resides in a dividend paying life insurance policy. We will examine the realities of how much of our income we give away without a whimper, as we are trained to do so, since birth it seems.

Joshua Thompson explains this succinctly in his book *"The Simple Banking System".* He states that the idea of banking is very simple. Don't be the reason the growth stops, be the reason it continues to grow. Your money should always be expected to grow. If you want to use that money, you should be required to keep it growing, and not be the reason it doesn't achieve its full potential. While you are accumulating the money, your money is growing. While you are using the money, your money is growing. By taking collateralized policy loans, we let our money compound uninterrupted with all the advantages of whole life insurance . That small difference adds up to a large advantage when it comes to retire or Financial Independence Day, as I prefer to call it.

We all save, then spend, save more, then spend again. Or conversely, get in debt, pay it off, get in debt then pay it off. The cycle repeats itself like the example below and this financial slavery does not end. In "Becoming Your Own Banker", Nelson Nash references Parkinson's Law. Parkinson's Law states that what were once luxuries, become necessities as soon as they can be afforded. So greater income results often in this saving and spending loop that causes the majority of the population to be stuck in such a consumption trap.

Individuals and companies have sinking funds to budget the purchases they hope to make in the near term and their future. What Joe Kane's sinking fund illustrates on the following page is, that you can't refute is that when you drain your sinking fund, you are not earning interest on that money. Your opportunity cost has worked against you. The simple problem with savings is when you deplete them, your money stops growing. This is not the case with Infinite Banking. The traditional way of purchasing items is a finite system. It is limited by the money you NEED to continue earning. The Infinite Banking system replenishes itself over time and you can use it over and over again. The more you use it, the more beneficial to your net worth. It is not get rich quick. It is save, borrow from YOURSELF, spend, pay yourself back and grow rich over time. Over the last ten years, the dividends from the life insurance companies I use have averaged seven percent. If I paid for my property taxes with my banking system, it would take me ten years to recapture the first year of property tax payment I made with this system. Albert Einstein's Rule of 72, simply states that to find out how long it takes to double your money, divide the compound interest rate you are earning into 72. On year eleven, I would recapture year two of payments and on year twelve, I would recapture year three of payments . This is because, the initial outlay I have paid back has doubled in value over these time periods. These examples are different for everyone, as we all have different circumstances and cash flows. This cash flow management system goes on and on and is only limited by your imagination and discipline.

Sinking Fund Illustration

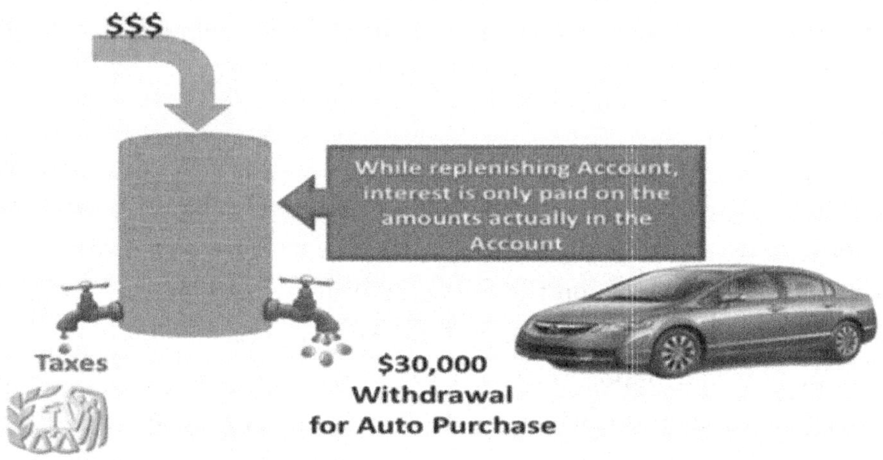

--Joe Kane: The Tank Conferences

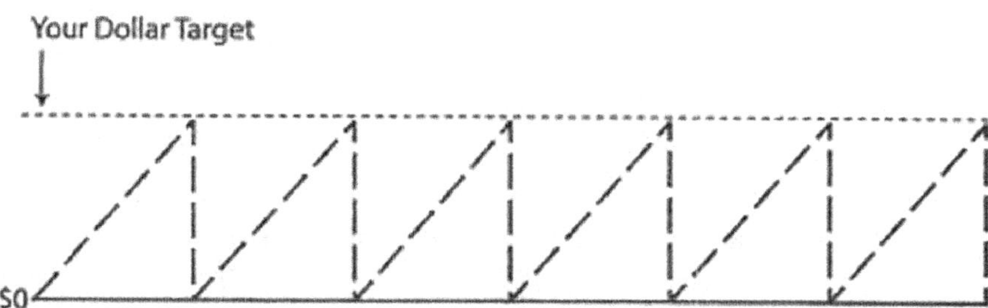

Figure 1—Balance in a savings account that is used periodically for major purchases

--"Bank on Yourself" by Pamela Yellen

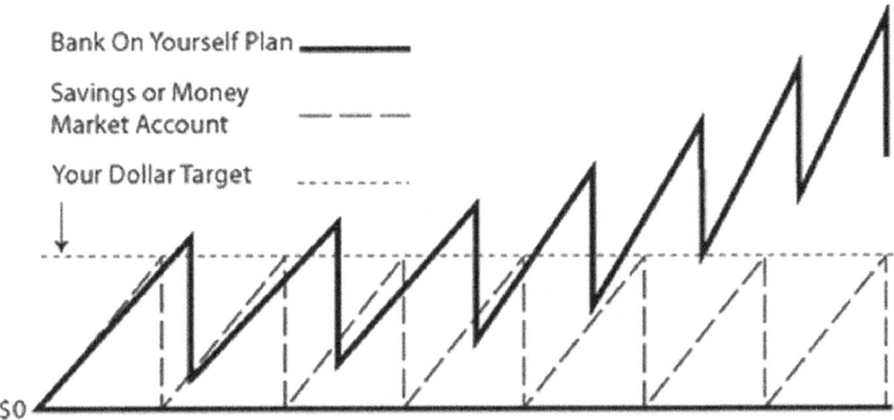

--"Bank on Yourself" by Pamela Yellen

Purchasing items, whether it's cars, equipment, or vacations through this program does not work against you. The account you are using as collateral (the cash value of your life insurance) is always growing, even if there is a lean against it, which is the loan to yourself. YOU are the banker.

This simple paradigm shift can add one million dollars to your net worth in your life time, simply by changing the way you purchase cars. Each time you deposit money in your bank account and then remove it, the bank stops paying you interest. This does not happen with your Infinite Banking System! See the diagram on the following page to understand how this works over a 30 year period.

PURCHASE AN AUTOMOBILE EVERY 5 YEARS BY PAYING CASH

Current Value of Assets:		Auto Purchase Frequency (yrs):	5		
Annual Savings:		Actual Purchase Price:	$45, 000		
Ann. Savings Increase (%):		Ann. Auto Price Increase (%):	3.00%		
Net ROR on Savings (%):	6.00%	Sales Tax Rate (%):	12.00%	Cumulative Auto Costs:	($579, 684)
Number of Years:	30	Ann. Auto Insurance Premium:	$1,500	Actual Asset Value WITH Auto Costs:	($1,290,040)
Year of First Purchase:	5	Ann. Insurance Increase (%)	3.00%	True Cost of Automobiles:	($1,290,040)

YEAR	Automobile Purchase	Sales Tax	Auto Insurance	Cumulative Auto Costs	EOY Asset Value WITH Auto Costs	Loss of Future Asset Value
1			(1,500)	(1,500)	(1,590)	(1,590)
2			(1,545)	(3,045)	(3,323)	(3,323)
3			(1,591)	(4,636)	(5,209)	(5,209)
4			(1,639)	(6,275)	(7,259)	(7,259)
5	(50,648)	(6,078)	(1,688)	(64,689)	(69,614)	(69,614)
6			(1,739)	(66,428)	(75,634)	(75,634)
7			(1,791)	(68,219)	(82,070)	(82,070)
8			(1,845)	(70,064)	(88,950)	(88,950)
9			(1,900)	(71,964)	(96,301)	(96,301)
10	(58,715)	(7,046)	(1,957)	(139,682)	(173,860)	(173,860)
11			(2,016)	(141,698)	(186,428)	(186,428)
12			(2,076)	(143,774)	(199,815)	(199,815)
13			(2,139)	(145,913)	(214,071)	(214,071)
14			(2,203)	(148,116)	(229,250)	(229,250)
15	(68,067)	(8,168)	(2,269)	(226,619)	(326,219)	(326,219)
16			(2,337)	(228,956)	(348,269)	(348,269)
17			(2,407)	(231,363)	(371,717)	(371,717)
18			(2,479)	(233,842)	(396,648)	(396,648)
19			(2,554)	(236,396)	(423,153)	(423,153)
20	(78,908)	(9,469)	(2,630)	(327,403)	(545,010)	(545,010)
21			(2,709)	(330,112)	(580,582)	(580,582)
22			(2,790)	(332,903)	(618,375)	(618,375)
23			(2,874)	(335,777)	(658,524)	(658,524)
24			(2,960)	(338,737)	(701,174)	(701,174)
25	(91,476)	(10,977)	(3,049)	(444,239)	(855,076)	(855,076)
26			(3,141)	(447,380)	(909,710)	(909,710)
27			(3,235)	(450,615)	(967,722)	(967,722)
28			(3,332)	(453,947)	(1,029,317)	(1,029,317)
29			(3,432)	(457,379)	(1,094,713)	(1,094,713)
30	(106,045)	(12,725)	(3,535)	(579,684)	(1,290,040)	(1,290,040)

As you can see, by buying a car every five years for thirty years, your cumulative cost (including insurance, tax and modest inflation) is $579,684. If you could earn 6% on your cash, these car purchases really cost you $1,290,040 in Loss of Future Asset Value over a 30 year period. The $1,290,000 number reflects the power of not allowing the growth of your capital to be interrupted. By paying cash, we destroy the capital. Infinite Banking cures this. By not interrupting the growth of your capital, you can turn your expenses into a growing capital base. The loans taken out by you are collateralized by this capital base. The loans, in turn, do not interrupt the growth of this capital base. Six percent has been a reasonable dividend to expect over the last 30 years from dividend paying life insurance.

You can think about this for many months or years and let the power of compound interests slip away or you can start this right away and do away with the banking system that is lending you your own money at rates much higher than they are paying you. Typing this sentence makes my head want to explode! I can't believe we have been conditioned to accept this slavery for so long without questioning it! Talk about manufactured consent! Thankfully, the choice is YOURS!

The next chapter will show how focusing on how much you keep, can trump focusing on a great rate of return without even focusing on the risk adjusted reality of one strategy versus another. When you adjust for risk, there is no comparison, if one is disciplined. This is because, even though there is a loan taken against your cash value in your policy, the collateral that facilitates the loan grows as if there was no loan there in the first place. The dividends, with a non – recognition company, get paid the same whether there is a loan or not. That is the often overlooked breakthrough. Incidentally that loan is payable to a company of whom you are a mutual owner. You benefit from the interest charged since your company has advanced the money to begin with. There is no underwriting questionnaire, as a contractual right warranted by the cash value in your policy, or private banking system, as we prefer to call it. It's simply how much for how long based on the amount you have capitalized the private banking system. The simplicity and importance of not losing the opportunity to earn money on your capital was never talked about in any of the dozens of financial planning textbooks myself and my colleagues where required to read. Beyond common sense, budgeting and earning a greater return on our savings, the cash flow management concept of Infinite Banking was never suggested.

When I studied Economics at the University of British Columbia, I came across this famous quote by Mark Twain: "*Never let formal education get in the way of your learning*". This comment offended me at the time as I was acquiring the "Arrival Syndrome" at a University that was going to make me elite just by attending it. Looking back now, I am embarrassed that I ever had such a belief. I didn't understand Mark Twain's comment then; Now after 15 years of learning and re-learning the way Alvin Toffler described in the 70's, I understand that like a 2 X 4 to the head.

Chapter 3

MAXIMIZE YOUR POTENTIAL WITH PRIVATE BANKING

"A clever person solves a problem. A wise person avoids it."
-Albert Einstein

In "Becoming Your Own Banker," Nelson Nash outlines what is obvious to everyone, once they give it some thought. We accept, without any fuss, systematically spending, losing and torching for good 90% or more of all the money we earn in a lifetime. We don't realize there is another way to go about one's finances. We have been told to accept this reality. On page 17 of Nelson Nash's book, he simply identifies "the problem". The reality of the matter is quite simple. The average North American spends 34.5% on interest, 30% on taxes (47.5% of Americans pay no income tax) and 25% or more on lifestyle. We hope to save and invest 10% of our earnings, however the average is sadly less than five percent.

When people gather around the water cooler or meet for coffee, their conversation is not about how to reverse the amount they pay in interest or changing the banking equation in their life. The conversation is typically about earning a higher rate of return on the miniscule amount of money they save for themselves or in obtaining a lower rate of interest they pay to some "other" bank. The true savers proudly talk about paying themselves first. This is great! Nelson Nash shone a laser beam on setting up a system where you pay yourself first into a vehicle that will reverse over time the financial headwind we all experience. Think for a minute; how much do you have to earn on your savings or investments to outperform the 60-95% loss you have accepted as a fate you can do nothing about? The return required is many fold higher than the 6-12% financial gurus are hired to hopefully achieve.

With the Infinite Banking solution, you can't reverse this financial slavery model overnight. However, by gradually moving what you have saved and continue saving to a system that replenishes itself with little or no risk, you can reverse the massive losses you experience in your spending by controlling the environment that you finance your expenditures with. What is a massive headwind financially, gradually turns into a massive tailwind as the madness is reversed and you transition from a Finite system to an Infinite system that replenishes itself over time. Nelson Nash points out the countless financial gurus that preach "getting out of debt". The gurus never address what the solution to permanently getting out of debt is. Becoming your own Banker is the obvious solution that cannot be ignored once you learn to look at your finances this way. It is the financial equivalent of the arrow in the FedEx sign we can never ignore once this reality has been pointed out to us. This paradign shift in cash flow management is the unique theme and message of the Infinite Banking concept. We will talk about the stages of this journey in Chapter Eight. It is not a get rich quick journey. It is a variation of the too good to be true statement "spend and grow rich". As you will see, it goes like this: save in an account that has averaged a seven percent return in the last ten years, borrow from yourself with zero hassle, spend, pay yourself back at a pace that is right for you and repeat over and over infinitely. Eventually, and this point in time is different for everyone, you can take a tax free income from this system that will replenish itself over time and leave a tax free legacy you can control.

CHAPTER 4

SPECULATION (ONLY WORKS CONSISTENTLY FOR INSIDERS)

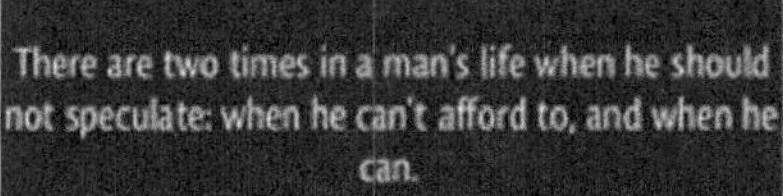

October. This is one of the peculiarly dan- gerous months to speculate in stocks in. The others are July, January, September, April, November, May, March, June, December, August, and February.

(Mark Twain)

I live in one of the venture market capitals of the world - Vancouver, British Columbia. In spite of the dismal success rate of ventures (98% fail within first ten years) I am amazed how much money is raised annually to fund ventures that hope to become sustainable companies. That is good for the economy and standards of living for the majority of the population. Many fail in this ongoing innovation odyssey that is a must for humanity's evolution. This is great for humanity. It is very likely, not right for you, personally. Most people will acknowledge that most companies don't make it and will not debate with you that one out of ten companies, at best, will survive longer than five years. For this reason alone, I admire the entrepreneur that puts everything on the line to serve the planet. What is problematic, however, is how mainstream these lottery tickets are purchased as sound financial independance strategies. Vancouver has recently had a resource boom/bust, that followed a technology.com bubble. The fact that money was invested here is not the real story. The real story is what percentage of people's net worth these investments are. I have seen individuals approaching retirement, have ¾ or more of their net worth in micro cap start ups or shares of companies, large or small, that have little or no earnings or revenue. The average sophistication of the individuals involved, is not surprisingly – modest. I have heard of many studies which point out that less than 9% of the population can read financial statements. For this reason alone, I always scratch my head on why individuals feel so confident about the stocks they own or want to buy when they rarely have the slightest clue about the fundamentals of the companies involved. Fundamentals like earnings, debt, book value, financial ratios, market capitalization, etc.

The point, I believe, which illustrates best why speculation is foolish, is the reality of the mirage of average financial returns. For example, if someone invests $100,000 and averages 25% a year. Are they really earning 25% a year ? From a calculator's standpoint, it might be 25% a year. If you walk through a simple financial example that I have painted by numbers below, you will see the FEDEX arrow that was there all the time. I have experienced these equity destroying round trips many times, and I refuse to participate in the insanity any more.

"Insanity: doing the same thing over and over again and expecting different results" –Albert Einstein

$100,000 investment	Year One Performance	+100%
$200,000 present value year two	Year Two Performance	-50%
$100,000 present value year three	Year Three Performance	+100%
$200,000 present value beginning of year four	Year Four Performance	-50%
$100,000 present value at END of year four	Average Performance	25%

Equity Gain = ZERO!

I can't speak for you, however, does this not look like your experience with penny stocks, for example?

Try the above with your calculator. It's simple and a reality I see or hear about over and over again.

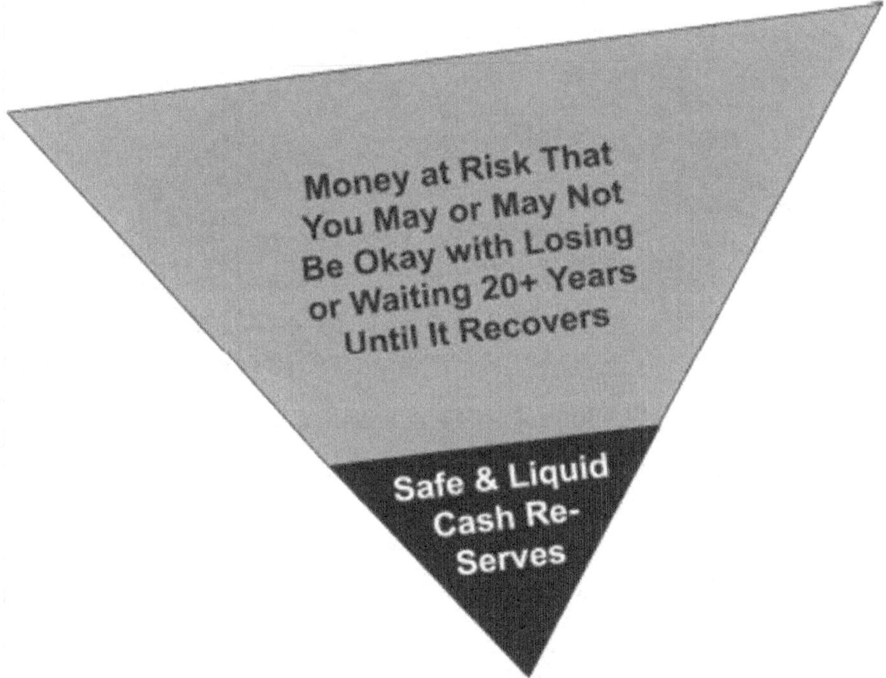

--"Bank On Yourself Revolution" by Pamela Yellen

The last 15 years have shown us that if your portfolio is made up of mostly equities and real estate, your portfolio resembles this unstable circumstance. "Bank on Yourself" allows you to have a foundation similar to the next diagram without getting low single-digit returns.

Because Life's a Lot Less Stressful When You're Working with a Financial Safety Net!

--"Bank On Yourself Revolution" by Pamela Yellen

The adversity of the last 15 years should ring the alarm bells to demand a portfolio with a stable high yielding foundation such as a dividend-paying life policy. Traditional equity investments can compliment this.

Of course, we tend to only remember our winners. I have been guilty of that. Perhaps we can all identify with that reality. We can learn from the adversity that others have gone through or let adversity repeatedly beat our net worth into the ground like the above example. I used to speculate to a degree that was unhealthy. I don't at all any more.

Warren Buffet's 2 simple rules to Investing:
Rule number 1. Never lose money
Rule number 2. Never forget rule #1

Below, I summarize the difference between an investment and speculation. To be clear; the money that resides in your personal private banking system is savings. When these savings are used to buy investments, we create superior performance, than if the investments were bought directly with cash, before it resides in your private banking system. The superior cash flow management attributes of Infinite Banking is what causes this improved performance on the same underlying investment.

John Maynard Keynes definition of investing: "Investing is the activity of forecasting the yield over the life of an asset; speculation is the activity of forecasting the psychology of the market".

One of the investment counsellors I work with- Dixon Mitchell has definitions for the two that clearly explain the difference. Speculation is buying an asset with the belief that someone will pay more for it than you did. Investing is buying an asset at a value which is justified by current cash flow generation and for which future cash flow growth will drive capital appreciation.

In summary, I believe the average individual is far better off saving through their dividend paying whole life policy. Once worthy investment opportunities are identified, the Private Banking System should be used to take advantage of these opportunities. See Chapter Nine, "Your Investments Will Perform Better with the Infinite Banking Concept" for more details. Speculation should be limited or not considered unless you are an insider, perhaps.

Chapter 5

"TERM AND INVEST THE DIFFERENCE" IT'S GREAT FOR WALL STREET, BUT, NOT FOR YOU!

"What we know is a drop, what we don't know is an ocean."
–Isacc Newton

Life insurance used to be sold as yearly renewable term. The problem with this was that only the sick would keep the coverage and healthy individuals would cancel their insurance as the premiums became prohibitive. The life insurance industry had a wonderful solution for those that did not want to budget for a permanent life insurance policy. This became know as 10-year or 20-year term insurance. A wonderful solution to maximize profits and cover people during the period of time they statistically had little or no chance of claiming, less than 1% to be exact. It is a well known fact in the industry that term insurance pays out less than 1% on average. This is a good thing as life expectancies have improved. Term insurance is better than no insurance.

This product structure, however, is not out of the goodness of the industry's heart. It is a brilliant profit margin protector. Cover people when they are young and extremely unlikely to claim and make it impossible to renew in the years that they are now much more likely to claim. Voila! – you never pay out and you have the masses investing into managed portfolios like mutual funds, wrap accounts and private pools therefore earning a fee whether the investment performs or not; quite a lucrative business model.

When the paradigm shift known as Infinite Banking hit me like a bus, I became furious. Why is everyone not doing this? The reasons are many. The most obvious one is this one: profit margins. As a rule of thumb, independent of profit margins, if everyone is doing something, there is not much opportunity left. You don't necessarily want to do what everyone else is doing. I knew this and calmed down when the welcome and amazing opportunity started to sink in. The poem "The Road Less Traveled" by Robert Frost artistically outlines this simple reality of not following the herd. In modern times, author of "Rich Dad Poor Dad," Robert Kyosaki highlights the fact that successful and financially independent people do explicitly the opposite of what most people are willing to do.

My discovery that 50-75% of savers used life insurance before the 80's inspired me to educate myself about what special interest or profit motives led to abandoning the age old savings solution known as dividend paying whole life insurance. How could we repeatedly overlook an asset class that hasn't performed poorly over the last 5, 10, 20, 50, 100 and 150 years, had zero risk, could provide policy or collateralized loans without requiring underwriting approvals, could provide the functions of a private banking system, could create guaranteed tax free income for life, could recapture lost interest and consumption expenses, and could do many other entrepreneurial functions that were generally only limited by your creativity? I knew many of these functions where independently available within whole life insurance. Why did it take over 150 years for a system known as Infinite Banking to finally be published? Why was it published only because of traumatic financial adversity? This adversity was solved with dividend paying life insurance.

The biggest answer, I believe, is a little advertised piece of legislation known as ERISA combined with special interest incentives that encouraged the financial lobbies to create one set of favoured financial solutions versus another. In this case "buy term and invest the difference."

I was a massive proponent of 'Buy Term and Invest The Difference' as a solution of choice for not all, but many financial circumstances. It works; however, it is generally inferior to integrating Infinite Banking with your whole cash flow management system. I will elaborate the specifics on how this cash flow management system works in chapters seven to ten.

Rick Bueter, a long time financial planner from the United States, highlights best the "Great American Retirement Experiment" in his words. After the post war stock market boom, Wall Street experienced a serious contraction in performance and ultimately revenue. Consumer confidence plummeted and Congress was concerned about a possible "domino effect" involving otherwise solvent brokers who had substantial open transactions with firms that failed. This is surprisingly reminiscent of of today's debacle and the sub-prime mortgage market.

But, Wall Street was still looking for a solution to regain footing and needed a catalyst to get the American investing public to start investing again. They found their answer by lobbying congress. The more things change, the more they stay the same, I guess.

The "Do-it-Yourself" Retirement Program begins in 1974 through heavy lobbying by Wall Street and businesses, Congress changed the retirement tax laws of America. They launched a new set of retirement plan rules called ERISA, the Employee Retirement Income Security Act. There were dozens of detailed changes with ERISA, but there are two that are critical and require a closer look.

The first is that of the vesting rules for Defined Benefit plans, the type of plans that told you what you could expect exactly, in retirement. The rules changed so that an employee receives a retirement benefit without the need to work nearly their entire life for the same company. This became a major challenge for pension managers who needed to restructure portfolio investments since benefits needed to mature sooner. Investments with shorter time horizons also caused diminishing investment returns. The shorter investment time horizon and shorter vesting schedules placed greater challenges on businesses. They now found that they had to put more money into a retirement plan at a time when the business environment was not very good. This was a disincentive for businesses to want to create a secure pension for their employees.

The second and most noteworthy aspect of ERISA was that it was the beginning of the Do-It- Yourself retirement system, also known as the Individual Retirement Account (IRA). To get Americans to buy into the new DIY retirement system, Congress created the incentive of a $ 1,500 tax deduction for the first IRAs. This new retirement system, called a "Defined Contribution System," would require lots of explanation. Americans now had to learn how to invest for retirement on their own. Up here in Canada, it was monkey see, monkey do, with a modest time lag. Our qualified plans have different names such as RRSPs, DPSPs, RESPs and TFSAs, etc.

So , who would step up to help Americans navigate their way through this new pension program? Who was desperate to find a new niche opportunity that was perfectly positioned to guide financially illiterate American workers with these new laws? Who had the financial solutions employees would need? It was Wall Street indeed...and they could not have been happier.

It was a new beginning for Wall Street and the key to regaining the trust of American investors. It was the spark that gave Wall Street the answers for which they were looking. They were now able to market to every American worker and help them fund their own retirement with stocks, bonds, and mutual funds.

The 401k was born. In Canada, think RRSP.

In 1980, Wall Street found their answer to becoming the gatekeeper of the American savings with the 401k plan. After successful launch of the Individual Retirement Account (IRA), Congress implemented the 401k. Now Wall Street could set up shop right at the employer's doorstep. This would give them control at the paycheck level using automatic payroll deductions. They knew that creating the tax incentive at the employee level and providing a turnkey system for businesses would be a powerful sales proposition for both the employer and the employee.

Funding a 401k in a financially unsophisticated manner with the majority held in one stock (your employer's stock perhaps) turned out to be a huge disaster for millions of Americans. Enron was probably the most well known company to disappoint their employees who had invested their life savings in its 401k's funded with company stock. More recently, GM, Nortel, AIG, Wachovia, Research in Motion and countless others have suffered the same fate. These were people who had worked a lifetime and lost it all in a flawed system they trusted to create retirement security. There are thousands of stories like these. I never want to be a part of this. Ever! I have never been and will continue to preach the same diversification theme going forward. Both in security selection as well as true asset class diversification.

The insurance industry has had their own interesting metamorphosis. Term insurance used to be exclusively annually yearly renewable term. In English this meant that the coverage would stay the same every year, however, the price would increase gradually over time. This works great in the beginning. The problem occurrs in the later years...15 years and beyond. What would start happening is that the coverage would only be kept by individuals who were in poor health. 15 years and beyond, many coverages would be viewed (as a result of a lack of financial education) as a discretionary expense and be cancelled. Your kids are likely not dependants after year 18 so only keep it if your health is not good. Big problem for the insurance companies. This is known as anti-selection. To make an insurance pool work, you had to have a majority stick with their coverage. In the case of yearly renewable term. The books of insurance companies were piling up with insureds who had a shorter life expectancy as a result of coverage only being renewed annually by people in below average health. This trended towards a naturally occurring anti-selection insurance phenomena.

The insurance companies had a brilliant solution: level term insurance for typical periods of 10 or 20 years for example. The rates would stay the same for 10 or 20 years, and then they would violently shoot up. Typically three times the original premium cost at the end of every term period.

As you can see, at the time you are becoming more likely to claim, you are likely to cancel. This is a very clever way to preserve margins at a successful insurance company. Term insurance pays out less than 1% of the time. Permanent insurance, such as whole life pays out 20% of the time. Still not good. This is a function of individuals not sticking to their long term financial plans, often as a result of poor service from their advisor, not necessarily a result of the quality of the plan in place.

So, in the last 40 years, we have had a massive shift from guaranteed defined benefit plans to defined contribution plans. These defined contributions took a fee whether or not they provided a guaranteed return, whether or not the performance adjusted for risk, and whether or not it was of quality. The margins on these fees are much higher than margins on plans that had to guarantee a payout and became a liability for the issuer. Few now want these liabilities.

At the same time, we have had a massive shift from permanent dividend paying whole life, that automatically made you an owner of the company (similar to a credit union) over to term insurance plans, that are massive profit centers for insurance companies, as they rarely pay out.

Many believe that these are the obvious reasons term and invest the difference became the predominant solution pushed by many financial intermediaries in the last 40 years. Get paid whether accounts went up or down and have no liabilities for an individual's retirements in tandem with having less than 1% of your liabilities pay out on the insurance. Its a profit protection plan that I believe is a financial wonder of the world. This is precisely why it must be part of the solution, instead of the problem that I see too often.

The antidote to these disappointing solutions (or doomed to fail financial plans) is guaranteed income for life that is one of the many benefits of the Infinite Banking system. Two of the many benefits that will be explained in greater detail in the following chapters.

There are wonderful firms like Vertex Asset Management and Dixon Mitchell that regularly add value by consistently beating their benchmarks NET of their fees. Quality firms like these deserve to be in your portfolio and form part of your financial independence. There are also quality insurance companies like Equitable Life and Manulife Financial that offer guaranteed income for life solutions in the form of Infinite Banking as well as guaranteed portfolio solutions.

Chapter 6

CENTRAL BANKS ARE NOT NECESSARILY FEDERAL

"Without big banks, socialism would be impossible"
-- Vladimir Lenin

Below is the Wikipedia summary of how the greatest fraud on earth works: Fractional Reserve Banking:

"Fractional-reserve banking predates the existence of governmental monetary authorities and originated many centuries ago in bankers' realization that generally not all depositors demand payment at the same time.

Savers looking to keep their valuables in safekeeping depositories deposited gold and silver at goldsmiths, receiving in exchange a note for their deposit (see Bank of Amsterdam). These notes gained acceptance as a medium of exchange for commercial transactions and thus became as an early form of circulating paper money. As the notes were used directly in trade, the goldsmiths observed that people would not usually redeem all their notes at the same time, and they saw the opportunity to invest their coin reserves in interest-bearing loans and bills. This generated income for the goldsmiths but left them with more notes on issue than reserves with which to pay them. A process was started that altered the role of the goldsmiths from passive guardians of bullion, charging fees for safe storage, to interest-paying and interest-earning banks.Thus fractional-reserve banking was born. However, if creditors (note holders of gold originally deposited) lost faith in the ability of a bank to pay their notes, many would try to redeem their notes at the same time. If in response a bank could not raise enough funds by calling in loans or selling bills, it either went into insolvency or defaulted on its notes. Such a situation is called a bank run and caused the demise of many early banks.

Starting in the late 1600s nations began to establish central banks which were given the legal power to set reserve requirements and to issue the reserve assets, or monetary base, in which form such reserves are required to be held. [6] The reciprocal of the reserve requirement, called themoney multiplier, limits the size to which the transactions in money supply may grow for a given level of reserves in the banking system. In order to mitigate the impact of bank failures and financial crises, governments created central banks – public (or semi-public) institutions that have the authority to centralize the storage of precious metal bullion amongst private banks to allow transfer of gold in case of bank runs, regulate commercial banks, impose reserve requirements, and act as lender-of-last-resort if any bank faced a bank run. The emergence of central banks reduced the risk of bank runs inherent in fractional-reserve banking and allowed the practice to continue as it does today"

The last sentence in this Wikipedia explanation is false because bank runs and other forms of bank insolvency still occur. Taxation has exploded since the creation of the Federal Reserve. The highest marginal rate when the Federal Reserve was created was 7%. Now it's north of 60% in California due to the collusion of bank and govermnent. Governments over spend and Central Banks print money to facilitate this. Interest on money that isn't backed by anything is charged. Slavery to banks that charge us on digitally made-up capital keeps us down. Infinite Banking is the antidote to fractional reserve banking. If you or I tried to lend money that was not backed by anything we would be thrown UNDER the jail!

Many believe the loaning out of money (that is essentially debt and does not exist as true capital) is fraudulent. This form of money creation has been responsible for the value of a dollar collapsing in a frightening way. It is my opinion that, done responsibly, this expansion of the money supply is not problematic beyond the gradual loss of purchasing power of the dollar. Unfortunately, there are many episodes like the Great Depression and more recently, the Sub Prime Crisis, where grave mistakes were made. The most famous free market economist, Milton Friedman stated that it was a massive mistake of the Federal Reserve that caused the Great Depression. This "mistake" was to lower the money supply by 30% and raise interest rates at a time where the economy needed stimulus, not catalysts that resulted in a deep freeze. Some cynics claim that this was not a mistake as more millionaires were created in the Great Depression than in any other time in history. The cynics claim this was deliberatly done to enrich a certain class of people. I am not in that camp...though I often wonder. After observing government for over thirty years, anything is possible.

Here is a link to a video of Milton Friedman talking about what caused the Great Depression : http://youtu.be/ObiIp8TKaLs

More recently, the easy money theme of the Federal Reserve advocated by Alan Greenspan led to the real estate bubble in the United States, central banks around the world generally did the same and we saw real estate trading at three standard deviations beyond what is historically normal. This is my favourite definition of a bubble: when the performance is three times more than what the historical fluctuation have been for that assett class. When the bubble started to unwind (all bubbles end when the factors that caused them reverses) the house of cards began to collapse. The history of the subprime crisis (which was described in Chapter One) unfolded and The Federal Reserve, the largest most powerful and sophisticated central bank in the world, failed to act as a lender of last resort.

The Federal Reserve was signed into law by Woodrow Wilson in 1913. It was a decision that he came to regret. The reason for this is that the Federal Reserve is not Federal. It is a cartel of private bankers that are supposed to act as lenders of last resort. *"The Creature From Jekyll Island"* by G. Edward Griffin is an account of the secret meetings that led to the forming of the Federal Reserve. It is a great read and will shine a light on why so many people attack the legitimacy of this private cartel of bankers.

What do I mean by lender of last resort?
Our banking system is a house of cards. This is because banks don't lend their money. They lend ours and that is fine. The fraud accusations result from the reality that our deposits in form of cash deposits, term deposits and savings accounts are their oxygen. With this oxygen, they are allowed to create money out of thin air in the form of debt and lend it back to us. When I connect the dots and show people the gross profit margins on this legal, leveraged carry trade or fraud if done in any other walk life, they start to see the fraud and the problems with fractional reserve banking.

The simple reality, that no one can deny, is a version of this scenario: You deposit your cash at the bank. The banks give you meager incentives that they claim are great to leave massive balances with them. Perhaps they give you an average of 1% on all cash residing with them. They then lend it back to you, your family, friends and everyone else in the economy at rates 2-18% higher, in the case of credit cards, than you are receiving. When I ask individuals what their gross margins are, the answer I get the majority of the time is 2-18 %. This is way off the mark for many reasons.

Remember the simple banking concept from the previous chapter? Banks don't lend their money: they lend other people's money. So in the scenario from the previous chapter, banks cost of money is one percent. This is what they pay you. They get at least three percent. Only their absolutely best clients get that rate; typically four to six percent or more for the majority of the population. So what is a two percent profit on money that cost you one percent? 200% gross profit! If you remember from a previous paragraph, they lend out much more than they have on reserve as deposits from me and you. It is legal to lend ten times their reserves and the central banks are the ones who authorize this. So 200% gross profit multiplied by ten at the extreme. This extreme is not likely for risk management reasons, however, you can now see hopefully why our economy has always been a house of cards. Now you can see why banks don't want to take over properties by foreclosure unless they absolutely have to. Its often better to take a loss and build up the balance sheet with the printing press known as fractional reserve banking. As we have recently seen in the US, they are willing to take massive losses so they can get back cash right away to make those amazing profits and rebuild their balance sheets. They're not interested in collecting measley rents when they can make those triple digit gross profit margins on their clients. How can banks afford to have a branch on EVERY commercial corner? Now you know how. We need strong and stable banks. I know for a fact that you don't need them for anything beyond a traditional checking account if you implement the Infinite Banking system. You also are better served if you work with a financial advisor who can represent you in the market place, all bank products included, instead of representing the bank and the limited options they have available in their branches. I will explain this in more detail in Chapter Nine.

The Federal Reserve is run by human beings. I don't need to patronize anyone by explaining that humans make mistakes. So you probably don't need much convincing that they will make massive mistakes or bad judgement calls in the future, simply because of the human factor. Perhaps these mistakes are not mistakes...perhaps they are deliberate attempts at legal theft. I am not a believer of that theory, however, I simply want to highlight the antidote to this house of cards.

The antidote is legal, private banking. The Infinite Banking system can create wealth by simply reversing where your interest payments are going, along with recapturing what you spend on everything large or small. This takes 5-15 years, however, when you do it over and over again and think long term, you will go from a finite system that depends on you going to work, to an infinite system that replenishes itself and provides guaranteed income for life, when you choose the reasonable time frame to do so. It is modestly different for everyone as everyone has different goals, dreams and means.

In addition to business titans like Walt Disney, Ray Kroc, JC Penney and Jim Pattison, it is a little known fact that the biggest purchasers of dividend paying whole life policies are BANKS! What better place to store your Tier One Capital if you were a bank. Tier One Capital is the capital that has to be the most liquid and safest on a bank's balance sheet.

Bank	**Life Insurance Assets**
Bank of America	$19,607,000,000
Wells Fargo Bank	$17,739,000,000
JP Morgan Chase Bank	$10,327,000,000
U.S. Bank	$5,451,892,000

--P.11- Money. Wealth. Life Insurance by Jake Thompson

There is no tax on the dividends a bank receives on their policies until the dividends match the total premium outlay or adjusted cost base of the policy. This does not happen for years. The dividends of the companies I use have averaged 6-8% over the last twenty years without missing a dividend payment, ever. Compare this to other liquid, safe options such as short term maturity treasury bills that pay 0.25 - 1% and you can see why the people that write the laws, lobbied by the banks themselves, are unlikely to make this wonderful vehicle disappear. Look up how much money banks donated to Barack Obama and other politicians. Government in Canada and the US have already severely restricted the amount you can put in to these tax advantaged, well-performing conservative vehicles. This is because they are the original Tax Free Saving Accounts! If you put policies on your Key

Employees and own the policies, you own the cash values and you own the policy's death benefit. An owner of an insurance contract can name any beneficiary and change it any time as well. It should come as no surprise that the banks name themselves as beneficiaries of these policies on their Key Executives. To their defense, they pay the premiums and there is an insurable interest here. Key Man life insurance is a Key Risk management tool in business and I help businesses put Key Man life insurance on their Key Employees all the time. There will always be a need for life insurance. It simply needs to be issued with the spirit of insurable interest - a death that results in a financial loss to the owner of the life insurance contract, whether it's a business or a family. This means, in non-financial gibberish, that there would be a tangible financial loss if the insured were to pass away. This can apply to a family or a business of course.

So, how are the dividends tax free for so long and rarely, if ever, missed? A dividend paying whole life policy premium is calculated on a level premium that is based on mortality tables and protects the insurance company from the one guarantee we humans all face in life. Conservative, high quality actuaries (math geniuses) figure out how much premium is needed in order to be able to pay claims from a company's reserves, in perpetuity, as well as provide a reasonable profit to shareholders of the company. I use a mutual company, which means simply, that the policy owners own the company in a similar fashion to how members own credit unions.

A good mechanical engineer will tell you where the red line is on the gauges of the equipment. You are warned that you are causing damage to the piece of equipment if you spend too much time in the red zone of the gauges. In reality, great engineers have been conservative in where the REAL red line is. You are able to go far beyond the red line in many circumstances, however, if you spend too much time there, as in the case of a plane, for example, bad things will happen. Similarly, in the case of a life insurance policy, an actuary will calculate the expected mortalities in a given year based on a ten million person sample size. Very conservative expectations are then determined regarding the financial performance of the investments made with the reserves of that company. Finally, premium calculations are made based on their WORST CASE scenarios for both of those key variables that are so crucial to the insurance business. In the last 150 years, it has been extremely rare to have both worst cases occur with well-established, highly regulated companies. At the end of the year, when the performance of the investments in reserve, along with the mortality experience of the company is tabulated, a dividend is declared which is the surplus that can be safely returned to the owners of the company tax free. With the companies I use, the policyholders are the owners of the company. I can use the whole market place. The legal technicality of this dividend is that it is a return of premium. They have charged you too much, hopefully, and this is the source of the dividend in the business of life insurance. Tax has already been paid on the premiums that have gone into the policy so that there is justifiably no tax owing on the dividend, as you have already paid tax corporately or personally on this money, up until the adjusted cost base of the policy. This is an example of how government has already sunken its teeth into the tax treatment of this vehicle. They have severely brought down the amount you can fund a policy with. It is not unlimited. It simply follows an insurable amount of life insurance that is reasonable, based on your earnings and net worth.

Chapter 7

DIVIDEND PAYING WHOLE LIFE INSURANCE: A LIVING BENEFIT

"Whenever you find yourself on the side of the majority it is time to pause and reflect"
—Mark Twain

My fifteen years of experience as a licensed life insurance professional had me focusing, the majority of the time, on the death benefit of life insurance. This was a financial planning reality that I embraced and is a sincere and genuine risk to have managed. One of the toughest professional experiences I have ever gone through is having a client pass away of whom I had recommended term life insurance to. She declined the coverage as she was confident in her mortality. She had two young daughters and was in great health. She passed away within a year of declining coverage with me. It was an accident and I had done my job. Everyday, insurance professionals are showing their clientele a better way to manage risk. I admire the work all professional life and disability insurance advisors are doing. It is not glamorous, however, it can make a massive difference in a family's financial well-being.

What frustrates me about the life insurance business, is the simple reality that the office employees that train new and existing agents, are not often aware of what a life insurance contract can do, beyond the death benefit. Nelson Nash first shone a light on this simple fact in the early 1980's when extreme adversity caused him to look for a solution to his 24% interest rate circumstance. This solution was staring at him the whole time, like the FEDEX arrow analogy. He was a licensed life insurance broker as well as a forester that was trained to think long term in terms of harvesting timber. Nash explains that after much praying and despair, the solution to his problem was staring him in the face all along. He could borrow, at much more favourable terms, from any of his three whole life policies that had significant cash values associated with them. This awakened him to what his industry training did not stress; the cash flow management capabilities and underwriting free loan feature of a dividend paying whole life policy. Today, when we speak of the living benefit of a life insurance policy, disability and critical illness insurance come to mind since that is what we have been told are living benefits. The psyche of life insurance in the marketplace is that you have to DIE to benefit from life insurance. That is the farthest thing from the truth. Ironically, the name says it all. LIFE INSURANCE, not DEATH INSURANCE! The living benefit, available in life insurance, can be accessed all the time, and by everyone, as I will show in Chapters Eight and Nine.

Whether it is using the cash flow management attributes within a dividend paying whole life policy, directing interest expenses to yourself rather than through a traditional bank, or funding the start of your great entrepreneurial enterprise, this is the ultimate living benefit. It does much more while you are alive than any other traditional living benefits named as such and has many more uses while you are alive than when a death claim is made. The understanding of this age old reality escapes the majority of financial professionals. I was one of them. My experience tells me that this is ubiquitous in the industry. This is not the fault of the advisors. I know first hand that most of the attributes of dividend paying whole life policies are not taught in the industry training curriculums. I don't believe this is a conspiracy. I believe it is the natural special interest evolution of defending the best business in the world - banking.

When looking at the makeup of a life insurance portfolio that I have displayed near the end of this chapter, you will see that 25% - 35% of a PAR accounts' (PAR account is the portfolio within a dividend paying life insurance company's book of investments that policy owners are a part of) portfolio, within a life company, is focused on a variation of the banking business. Whether it's commercial or residential mortgages, policy loans, or financing small business, in the private placement category of their participating account, why would an industry teach everyday people and the business they are patrons of, to compete against them? This is more common sense based than conspiracy based, I believe.

To summarize, for too long the death benefit was what was emphasized in life insurance by most agents. Death benefits are extremely important in financial planning. Term Insurance is better than no life insurance. The power of the cash value, in terms of being a liquid living benefit, was and still is extremely understated. I was a party to this not too long ago. The overwhelming majority of the industry still is. The compensation for the death benefit is much higher than the compensation for the cash value accrual. This is another non-technical reason for this bias I'm afraid. The second major reason is that the office employees of the life insurance companies don't know the positive and life-changing benefits of how to use your cash values as a private banking system that can recapture interest expense, depreciation or loss of your consumption dollars and make you a better investor in investments of any kind. If you're a sophisticated investor, cash flowing investments work best with the Infinite Banking system. Chapter Nine will demonstrate this more thoroughly.

On the following two pages is a testimonial from one of the most successful businessmen in Canada, Jim Pattison, explaining about how grateful he is for the "Living Benefit" of life insurance.

CORPORATE OFFICE, 18TH FLOOR, 1067 W. CORDOVA ST., VANCOUVER, B.C., CANADA V6C 1C7

JIM PATTISON
Chief Executive Officer,
Managing Director

December 4, 2012

Alberto Storelli

702 – 543 Granville Street
Vancouver, BC V6C 1X8

Dear Mr. Storelli:

This letter is in response to your request to me for a testimonial letter stating how the " Living Benefits " of Life Insurance helped me.

Through personal experience I discovered that life insurance has other assets in addition to protection of ones present or future family.

The business world, I discovered, has an interest in Life Insurance. Much of the world's business is carried on by credit, and bank applications for a line of credit are accompanied by, as a rule, a statement of affairs which requests information as to the amount of life insurance carried.

When I decided to open my first business which was a General Motors automobile dealership franchise at the corner of 18th & Cambie, I discovered a " Living Benefit " of life insurance, that of borrowing collateral.

When I approached the Royal Bank of Canada for additional capital, the cash values in my life insurance policies were a valuable asset that the Bank manager used in determining whether or not a loan would be granted.

If it wasn't for the cash values in my life insurance policies the bank may have decided against granting me the necessary capital to begin my first business endeavour.

I am certainly an advocate of life insurance as a vehicle to help a young person take advantage of business opportunities that may present themselves in the future.

It happened to me, and if could happen to others.

I am grateful for the " Living Benefits " of life insurance.

You have my permission to use this letter in your sales presentation.

Jim Pattison

The following three pages are taken from a marketing brochure created by Equitable Life of Canada:

HOW PARTICIPATING PREMIUMS ARE INVESTED

The amount of premium that is not required to pay for current benefits and expenses is invested in the participating account to provide for future benefits.

Participating account portfolio – asset classes
(As of December 31, 2013)

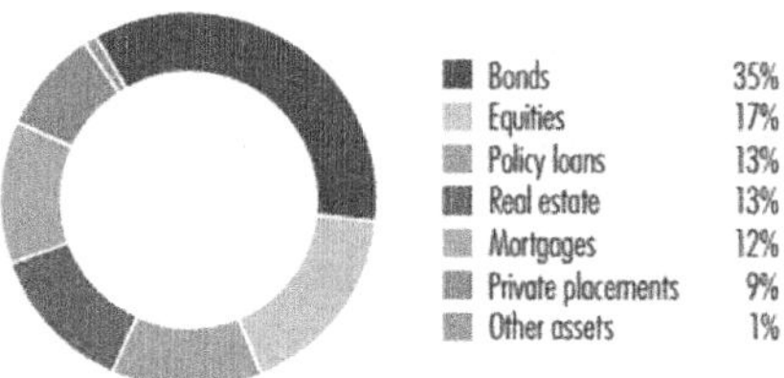

Participating account portfolio – details
(As of December 31, 2013)

		$ Thousands	Percentage
Short-term			
Cash and equivalents	$	85	<1%
Total short-term	$	85	<1%
Fixed income			
Government bonds	$	55,512	18%
Corporate bonds	$	55,314	17%
Private placements	$	27,577	9%
Commercial mortgages	$	38,341	12%
Total fixed income	$	176,743	56%
Non-fixed income			
Real estate	$	40,094	13%
Common equity	$	39,540	13%
Preferred equity	$	16,242	4%
Total non-fixed income	$	95,876	30%
Total invested assets	$	272,705	86%
Policy loans	$	40,194	13%
Other assets	$	3,302	1%
Total participating assets	$	316,200	100%

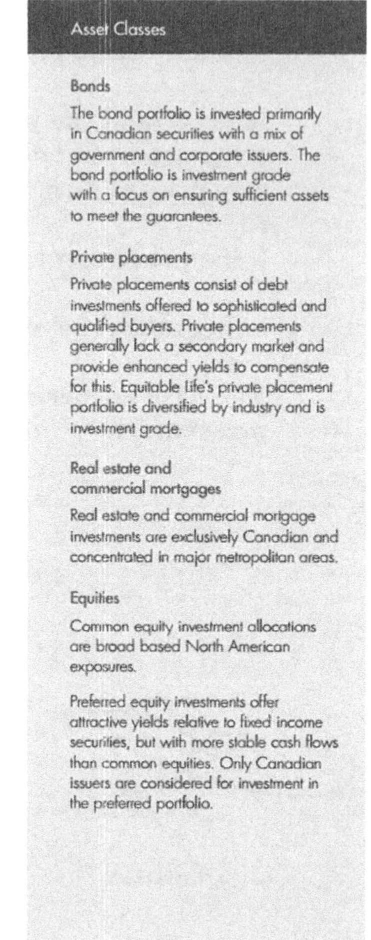
Asset Classes

Bonds

The bond portfolio is invested primarily in Canadian securities with a mix of government and corporate issuers. The bond portfolio is investment grade with a focus on ensuring sufficient assets to meet the guarantees.

Private placements

Private placements consist of debt investments offered to sophisticated and qualified buyers. Private placements generally lack a secondary market and provide enhanced yields to compensate for this. Equitable Life's private placement portfolio is diversified by industry and is investment grade.

Real estate and commercial mortgages

Real estate and commercial mortgage investments are exclusively Canadian and concentrated in major metropolitan areas.

Equities

Common equity investment allocations are broad based North American exposures.

Preferred equity investments offer attractive yields relative to fixed income securities, but with more stable cash flows than common equities. Only Canadian issuers are considered for investment in the preferred portfolio.

Above is a conservative, diversified portfolio that comprises a dividend-paying whole life policies' participating account. The dividend pay of these policies is achieved according to the performance of this conservative portfolio combined with the mortality experience of the insurance company.

HOW THE PARTICIPATING ACCOUNT RESPONDS TO MARKET CONDITIONS

During periods of high interest rates, the rate of return of the participating account tends to increase. During periods of low interest rates, the rate of return tends to decrease. The participating account return is also affected by equity markets, real estate markets, and corporate defaults. There is frequently a timing difference which results in less overall fluctuation in the rate of return on the participating account compared to assets in these markets and changes in the interest rate environment.

The following shows the historical returns of Equitable Life's participating account, net of investment expenses, compared to other well-known economic indicators.[4]

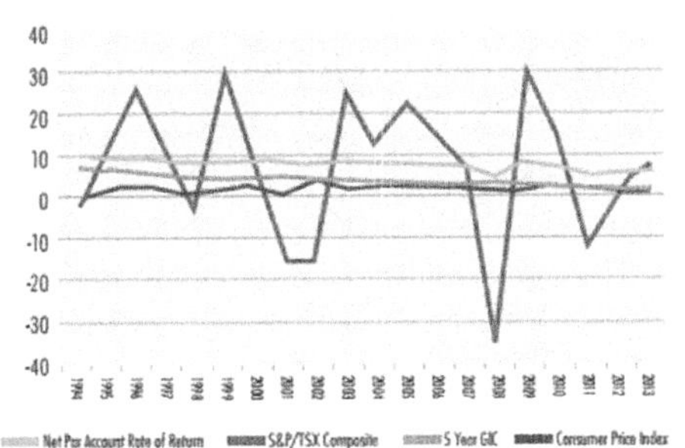

Year	Net Par Account Rate of Return	S&P/TSX Composite Index	5 Year GIC	Consumer Price Index
1994	9.6	-2.5	7.4	0.2
1995	9.4	11.9	7.1	1.8
1996	9.1	25.7	5.6	2.2
1997	8.5	13.0	4.7	0.8
1998	8.3	-3.2	4.4	1.0
1999	8.2	29.7	4.8	2.6
2000	8.2	6.2	5.3	3.2
2001	7.7	-13.9	4.0	0.7
2002	8.0	-14.0	3.9	3.8
2003	7.7	24.3	3.1	2.1
2004	7.6	12.5	2.9	2.1
2005	7.5	21.9	2.7	2.1
2006	7.6	14.5	3.2	1.7
2007	7.3	7.2	3.3	2.4
2008	4.9	-35.0	3.0	1.2
2009	8.6	30.7	2.0	1.3
2010	7.8	14.4	2.0	2.4
2011	6.0	-11.1	1.9	2.3
2012	7.3	4.0	1.7	0.8
2013	8.5	9.6	1.6	1.2
Average Annualized Returns				
1	8.5	9.6	1.6	1.2
3	7.3	0.8	1.7	1.4
5	7.7	9.5	1.8	1.6
10	7.3	6.9	2.4	1.8
20	7.9	7.3	3.7	1.8
Standard deviation since 1994	1.1	16.7	1.7	0.9

Note above the net participating account rate of return. Zero down years and a twenty year average of 7.9%. The fluctuation annually known as standard deviation is only 1.1% vs. 16.7% for the TSX. 2008 is of particular interest regarding performance versus the TSX (which is the return of a widely followed basket of Canadian stocks)

DIVIDEND SCALE INTEREST RATE

The dividend scale interest rate is just one factor used to determine the dividends paid in a participating policy. It is not the same as the participating account rate of return. The rate of return of the participating account goes up and down based on the economy. The dividend scale interest rate smooths out the ups and downs experienced by the participating account.

Here is a summary of our current and previous dividend scale interest rates:

Year	Dividend scale interest rate
1995	10.2%
1996	9.6%
1997	10.0%
1998	9.1%
1999	8.8%
2000	8.8%
2001	8.8%
2002	8.8%
2003	8.4%
2004	8.2%
2005	8.2%
2006	7.9%
2007	7.9%
2008	7.9%
2009	7.4%
2010	7.1%
2011	7.1%
2012	6.8%
2013	6.8%
2014	6.8%

The current dividend scale interest rate is effective for the period of July 1, 2014 to June 30, 2015.

Note the tax free dividend performance of the mutual company we use and the healthy tax-free dividend of 2008 and 2009 when economics were reeling. The dividend is derived from the company's investment portfolio returns combined with mortality performance (how many people claimed a death benefit). The mortality trends have improved one year per decade for the last 100 years. Leading futurist and theoretical physicist, Michio Kaku, believes life expectancy will improve one year per year within 30 years. He discusses this in the following YouTube video: http://youtu.be/_UgE-NhcmbM

Chapter 8

THE STAGES OF USING YOUR CASH VALUES AS THE ULTIMATE LIVING BENEFIT

"Twenty years from now you will be more dissapointed by the things that you didn't do than by the ones you did do..."
–Mark Twain

Unfortunately, the majority of people view life insurance as a necessary evil or a place where money is in prison until death. This stigma naturally exists because you have to die and someone else gets the benefit besides you; or even worse, you pay for decades and nothing comes back from the insurance companies. Nothing is farther from the truth and sadly the financial planning community is to blame, not the advisors.

I can attest to this and I am angered and frustrated that this strategy was kept as an afterthought as a financial planning tool. I view many of the required financial planning courses as money grabs for this very reason. All professionals, financial or not, can relate to the monopoly our educating bodies have in controlling what is relevant versus what is not. Everybody knows monopolies are bad. Even though over half a million Infinite Banking plans have been started in North America, it should be no surprise that this has not become more mainstream due to special interest involvement.

The undeniably flexible and liquid attributes of a dividend paying life insurance policy are so valuable that almost everyone should own one for their benefit. The word "own" is very important. The policy does not necessarily need to be on yourself, but rather that you own and control it. You can own insurance on anyone that you have an "insurable interest" in- a child, a business partner, a Key Employee or anyone else so close to you that if they died, you would be affected. This enables anyone, healthy or not, to benefit from this life changing concept.

The cash value and death benefit are controlled by the owner 100%, not the individual being insured. The Cash Value is 100% liquid. You, being the owner, can use both the cash value and the death benefit while you are living and they work like equity in real estate - with one major exception: they can never go down, only up.

Phase 1- The Start-Up Phase (Years 1 - 5)

This is the hardest part, deciding that you want to adopt this more effective, but less well-known, way of handling your finances. It's like starting a business; not only do you have to work against the nay-sayers, but you have to write cheques and more cheques and only then do you see any benefit.

During this phase, you are converting cash to cash value plus a death benefit. Both can provide a tax free income when used properly. Both are wonderful things to have, but hard to start. However, one start-up (though you may have many) equals a lifetime of benefits.

It's important to remember that *"...you finance everything you buy."* This quotation from Nelson Nash, author of *"Becoming Your Own Banker"*, indicates the accurate but rarely discussed fact that you either pay interest to someone for the use of their money or you give up interest you could have earned by using your own money. Life insurance gives you a way to more effectively finance the things you buy.

Phase 2- The Leverage Opportunity Phase and Investment Capability Phase (Years 6-30)

This is the enabler phase. It can begin as early as year two or as late as you like. Life insurance enables you to make better use of the game of financing (cars, vacations, etc.) as well as to make better investment decisions. Now that you are past the start-up phase, you can see that every dollar you put into your policy is turning into more than one dollar of cash value. This gives you opportunities for leverage and capabilities for investments.

Phase 3- Spending Other Assets (Years 20-40)

This is the cross - over between Part 1 and Part 2, between using your cash account to borrow against and using your death benefit to borrow against. Typical ages of those insured during this phase are the 60's, 70's and 80's, and how you use your life insurance at this point will depend on how long you have had it, as well as how many dollars are currently borrowed against it.

Phase 4 - Using the Death Benefit or Face Value of Policy (Years 41-50)

There are several ways you can use your death benefit or face amount while you are living . These can be combined or used as stand-alone strategies. It is interesting to note that life insurance helps people from a wide variety of financial backgrounds. For modest income earners, the premium payments become an important strategy for forced savings. Also, medium income earners end up with more dollars saved outside the policy because of the account flexibilty and the lack of a financial roller coaster impacting them. Lastly, life insurance helps those with larger amounts of money as they head into retirement age by enabling them to spend their own assets more efficiently. This last group could have $1 million or $1 billion, but the concepts are still the same.

Phase 5- Setting Up the "Family Bank" (Years 51+)

Ideally, you will die late in life with (1) most of your assets used up, and (2) your entire net worth, at its highest point, paid to your family and charities in the form of an income tax-free death benefit from the life insurance you own.

With proper estate planning documentation, this lump sum of cash could create a "family bank " whereby your grandchildren and great-grandchildren could borrow sums of money to pursue opportunities. This is the way wealthy families stay wealthy for generations: they replace their assets at each generation's passing and buy life insurance at each baby's birth.

How specifically you wish to design your family bank is up to you. The legal document itself that governs the family bank is generally a changeable trust until you die, at which point it becomes irrevocable. You can also leave specific amounts of the death benefit to charity or particular family members based on your desires.

Chapter 9

YOUR INVESTMENTS WILL PERFORM BETTER WITH THE INFINITE BANKING CONCEPT

"Nothing will ever be attempted if all possible objections must first be overcome."
–Samuel Johnson

The "Arrival Syndrome" also robbed me of having my investments performing better. I have been a licensed and registered financial advisor for fifteen years. I knew how to get ahead. These whole life plans that earn 7% tax-free are embarrassing if you want financial independence, right? I knew that if I compounded money at a higher rate of interest, I would shatter this performance long term. Sadly, every day, I come across financial and accounting professionals that have this limited mind set. And if the industry has it, what do you think the population's consciousness has? If things are repeated over and over again no matter how ridiculous, they will be accepted as fact. Consent was manufactured in the media like Noam Chomsky has warned for so long. Consent is manufactured in the media and in the financial planning textbooks that we are all forced to take, by the monopoly that is the financial education system. The media and financial services education bias is diametrically opposed to Infinite Banking. History shows that this is an important clue that special interest has become involved. If you review the facts of what the best business in the world is and how lucrative banking is, you will understand why we were not shown what has been there for over 150 years. The FedEx arrow has been there the whole time as well.

If you understand the simple difference between investments and saving, you will understand the missing link to the attraction to Infinite Banking and how it allows your investment to perform better. This is a simple function of the cash flow management and qualities of Infinite Banking. The simple difference between savings and investments is this: investments have risk and savings do not.

A dividend paying life insurance policy is safe, has guaranteed growth, competitive rates of return, and is not affected by emotional swings of market valuations and fundamentals. It is most analogous to a high interest savings account. Dividend paying whole life insurance vehicles are high interest saving accounts. Plain and simple. This is why it is so confusing to talk about these savings vehicles in comparison to stocks, bonds, real estate, mutual funds or any other investment. It is the proverbial comparing apples to oranges.

The most common question I get is: How do we get money from our life insurance company without liquidating the account and interrupting the growth of the cash value? The answer is simple: the life insurance company gives you access to loans against your policy equity (or cash values).

The loan rates will vary as the dividend rates vary, however, let's use a 7% loan interest rate and a 5% growth rate on the property or stock we wish to purchase. This property or stock also has a 4% dividend or net operating income from rent.

NO LOAN ON $100,000 CASH INVESTMENT
GROSS YIELD $9,000 → $5,000 APPRECIATION + $4,000 DIVIDEND
LESS TAXES @ 40% TAX BRACKET → $2,600 ($1,000 CAPITAL GAIN, $1,600 TAX ON DIVIDEND)
NET YIELD → $6,400 WITH NO LEVERAGE FROM DIVIDEND PAYING POLICY

So, how does Infinite Banking improve on that $6,400 profit without adding risk? The math works as follows: $100,000 is borrowed. Policy owner is in a tax bracket of 40%. The loan interest is $7,000. This is $4,200 after tax deductions. The $5,000 appreciation is $4,000 after tax. The dividend is 2.4% after tax conservatively. You also have simultaneously received a dividend from a life insurance company of 6% tax-free.

The cost of borrowing $4,200 net and your profit on the investment is $4,000 net capital gain after tax plus $2,400 net rental income after tax, for a total of $6,400. Your net profit is only $2,200 ($6,400-$4,200) after the tax cost of borrowing. Doesn't look very good does it? What we forget quickly is that there is another system working for you. Your banking system! You are the banker and your bank has paid dividends north of 6% for the last 30+ years! Your total profit is actually $8,200 vs. $6,400. This is a conservative example of how using your Private Banking System allows your investments to perform better without adding any risk! For the same investments you add an extra 28% to your return on investment. We obtain this number by subtracting $8,200 - $6,400 = $1,800. Then you divide $1,800 into $6,400 and you get .28125 X 100= 28.125%

WITH LOAN FROM BANKING SYSTEM

BORROWED $100,000 FROM POLICY

GROSS YIELD $9,000 → $4,000 NET APPRECIATION + $2,400 NET DIVIDEND = $6,400 NET YIELD

LESS INTEREST PAID (TO BANKING SYSTEM) $7,000 ($4,200 NET AFTER TAX COST)

TAXABLE GAIN $9,000

LESS TAX $2,600

NET YIELD → $2,200 ($6,400 AFTER TAX PROFIT - $4,200 AFTER TAX INTREST COST)

PERFORMANCE INCLUDING BANKING SYSTEM DIVIDEND

NET YIELD FROM INVESTMENT $2,200

(DIVIDEND) FROM BANKING SYSTEM + $6,000

TOTAL YIELD AFTER TAX (USING INFINITE BANKING SYSTEM) $8,200

This is the value added on an average investment scenario. The real power is the power to act quickly when you come across a distressed piece of real estate or wish to act quickly on an opportunity with a mispriced security or a straight out market crash that has not and will not affect the cash value of your Private Banking System. The greatest returns obtained by investors are returns that result from the value investing principles taught by greats such as Warren Buffet.

Infinite Banking amplifies your ability to buy when the average investor is fearful and the greatest bargains can be had quickly without wondering if the institution or bank you work with facilitates the loan required to pounce on a life-changing piece of real estate, as an example. As a result of the boom and busts created by the mismanagement of the central banks around the world, there will be more busts that will create amazing opportunities. Infinite Banking allows you to earn a strong return while you look or wait for these life changing opportunities.

Chapter 10

THE PROBLEMS WITH GOVERNMENT SAVINGS AND RETIREMENT PLANS

"If you tell the truth, you don't have to remember anything"
—Mark Twain

It is shocking to see the cost of post secondary-education. I believe in education and pride myself in being a lifelong learner and count my university days as some of the best of my life. Is it necessary for everyone to go to college? That is up for debate. Is it necessary to have our children come out of college with $ 50,000 - $ 100,000 worth of debt? Absolutely not!

A typical circumstance I encounter when I meet clients is one that goes something like this. A family has invested or saved money in their qualified retirement plans. The savings is often quite substantial. The problem is two fold, however; the money is in prison in a registered retirement savings plan or can't be replenished if it's paid for by an RESP or with cash. Debt is an ugly circumstance in most cases, obviously.

Finding out your child got accepted to a top-notch university or is about to get married is one of the most exciting things parents can ever go through.

After the initial excitement wears off, the financial reality hits quite hard. The parents are approaching their pre-retirement years. The mortgage still needs to be paid off and if you live in a city, cost of living is only going up. Society tells us we have to max fund our RRSP's and take risks in order to retire. This, however, is completely false.

RRSP's and RESP's are better than no savings at all. What if there was a better way to save for retirement, for your children's university tuition, and for your child's wedding, for example? These are major expenses that are some of the most important and fulfilling you will ever experience in life. We have been trained to store most of our savings and investments in government retirement and education plans. These plans can serve their purpose but there are some massive problems with these plans. The largest one is that your money is effectively in prison. What do I mean by that? We are happy to contribute dollars into these programs because the government is giving us a "tax break". However, if we need money for life's positive and negative surprises, how problematic is it having all or most of our eggs in this basket? RRSP contributions allow a write-off on your current taxable income. That is great. However, as the mechanic might tell you politely, you can pay me now...or you can pay me much more later. This is similar to the story about taxing the harvest or the seed. If you tax the seed, the greater bounty of the harvest will possibly be exempt from a much larger tax bill. The simple question to ask is what would you like to be taxed; the seed or the harvest? In the case of RRSP's, I suspect that for many people, you could possibly be much better off if you had the harvest free and clear of a tax structure that was as onerous on the back end as current RRSP structures are. Everyone's circumstance is a little different. The next concept will not be a little different for middle class or successful, hard working savers that are piling all their investments/savings into a vehicle such as RRSP's . The key lies in the control of that tax rate when you withdraw, combined with the history of leaders involved with determining that tax rate. No one I speak to in the business world on a daily basis, believes now, that tax rates are going down. In fact, the history of tax rates is quite shocking as you will see on the following page.

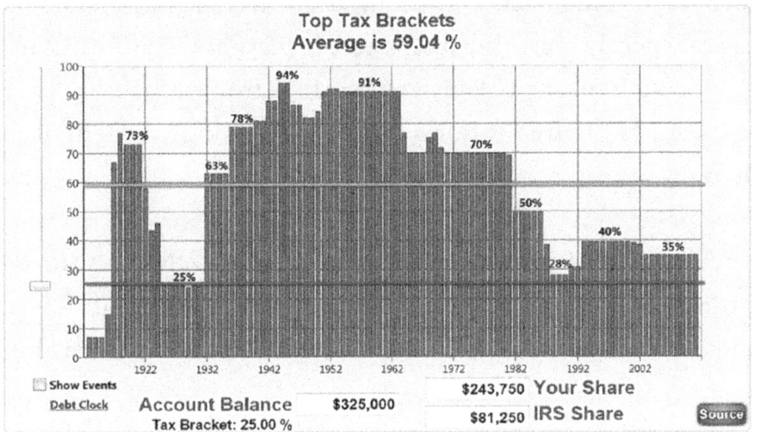

1062 *CANADIAN TAX JOURNAL / REVUE FISCALE CANADIENNE*

Table 3 Combined Federal and Provincial[a] Marginal Income Tax Rates for Selected Years and Selected Nominal Income Levels, 1949 to 1994

Taxable income	1949	1971	1972	1986	1987	1994[b]
dollars			*percent*			
1	15	0.00	21.68	8.82	9.00	26.35
1,001	17	21.76	24.23	8.82	9.00	26.35
3,001	19	25.00	26.78	24.99	25.50	26.35
5,001	22	28.00	29.33	26.46	25.50	26.35
7,001	26	26.00	31.88	26.46	27.00	26.35
9,001	30	30.00	34.43	27.93	28.50	26.35
11,001	35	35.00	39.53	27.93	28.50	26.35
15,001	45	45.00	44.63	45.60	30.00	26.35
25,001	50	50.00	49.73	53.38	37.50	26.35
40,001	59	55.00	54.83	53.38	45.00	40.30
60,001	64	60.00	59.93	53.38	51.00	46.40
90,001	69	65.00	59.93	53.38	51.00	46.40
125,001	74	70.00	59.93	53.38	51.00	46.40
225,001	79	75.00	59.93	53.38	51.00	46.40
400,001	84	80.00	59.93	53.38	51.08	46.40

Source: *The National Finances, 1985-86* (Toronto: Canadian Tax Foundation, 1986), 101, and *The National Finances, 1994* (Toronto: Canadian Tax Foundation, 1994), 7:7.

[a] The provincial rates are assumed to be 30.5 of the basic federal tax in 1972, 47 percent in 1986 and 1987, and 52 percent in 1994. [b] Owing to the refundable goods and service tax credits and child tax benefits, the 1994 rates for the lower income levels are not comparable to those of earlier years.

Note how high marginal tax rates were in the US and Canada in the 60's and 70's. I don't believe we're going back to 80-90% top marginal rate. I do believe we're going back to the long term average of 60% top marginal rate. France recently increased its top rate to 75%, and California increased to 60%. Infinite Banking shields your savings from this future problem as you can create a tax free income from your Banking System, if properly structured.

This concept is key to understanding why relying exclusively on a RRSP/RPP pension plan could be quite hazardous to your financial well-being and standard of living. I believe it is a variation of the road to serfdom. Here is why:

One of my mentors, Mary Lyons, describes our potenially frightening future as follows: "We're going into business together. You put up all the money. You take all the risk. You make many or most of the business decisions. In thirty years, I'm going to be the one who decides how much of the business you own. Would you still like to go into business together?" Sounds a little silly, until you realize the perfect RRSP analogy that this business question represents.

If you are still not convinced there needs to be alternatives considered, please note the history of tax rates in the US and Canada. When I show this to people, they are shocked to learn that in the 1960's the TOP marginal tax rates in the US and Canada were 80-90%! John F. Kennedy started the trend of lowering them. He was the modern godfather of supply side economics, of which I am a big fan of. Supply side is simply leaving more money is the hands of consumers as they know better what to do with the money as opposed to government who has little incentive to do the most intelligent thing with it. Far too often they are buying votes and torching our money, for their benefit. If you think I'm nuts, I invite you to check out Peter Schweizer's new book, *"Extortion: How Politicians Extract Your Money, Buy Votes and Line Their Own Pockets."*

I long for the day when a modern Cincinnatus comes to serve for purely virtuous reasons. Better organizes government and then leaves government on his own volition. If you don't know the story of the great Roman consul that had the city of Cincinnati named after him, I invite you to look it up on Wikipedia. The story will be somewhat close to what really happened. Always mindful of the lies agreed upon that history books represent.

To quote Henry Adams, "No man should be in politics unless he would honestly rather not be there." It's an ugly business. The word 'politician' comes from the Greek word 'poli', which means many. You know what a 'tic' is. Politics. Tough theatre to watch and observe. I would not do well here. The electoral masses, I find, can't handle truth. They prefer the "lies agreed upon."

This tax history picture below is a future nightmare waiting to happen, in my honest opinion. Note the average marginal tax rate of the last 100 years is 60%. In Canada, the rate is currently about 45% and a little lower overall in the US. Where do you think tax rates are going to trend to in both Canada and in the US as the largest generation in history approaches retirement and starts to collect on mass what unaccountable politicians promised them to get elected, many decades before? I believe the entitlement era is going to look a lot different than what was promised. Few disagree with me on this point for good logical reason. People are living longer and these programs are underfunded and will not be able to deliver on these promises.

Two things will happen, I feel. First, with the stroke of a pen, these entitlements will be pushed out to later years. Simultaneously, the top tax rates will trend back to the average of the last 100 years. This now brings me back to circle to the problem with getting a 43% tax break and then possibly facing the problem of having you or your estate pay over 60%. If you are still not convinced of the risk of government telling you how much THEY own of your business, in this case your retirement savings, look into what

France did in the summer of 2012. They raised the top marginal rate to 75%! This is not a dictatorship, right? The road to serfdom is creeping into too many parts of the world I fear. Infinite Banking is a hedge or antidote to this reality.

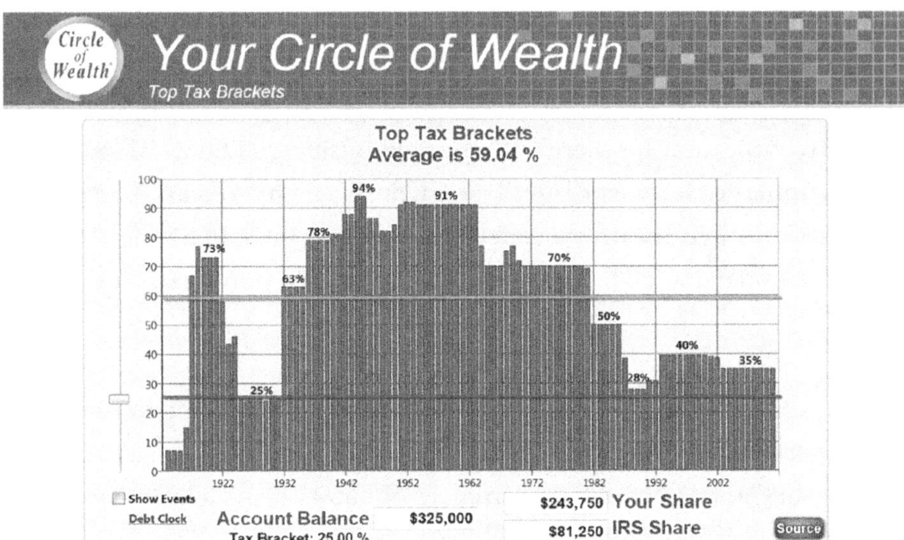

The argument I get on this reality is "you take out money when you are not working so that you will be at a lower marginal rate overall." This obviously can be very true for some. The problem is, if you pass away before life expectancy and the whole RRSP goes on your final tax return, then you are the government's best friend. If you have a one million dollar RRSP, are single or divorced, and pass away at age 70 and the tax rates have trended back to the average, your estate would be left with less than half.

The simplest way to think about this is to consider your million dollar RRSP and ask yourself, how much is mine? At best, it's around 60% right now. I feel it will be less than half in the future. Yes, if you do good things with the tax return, which effectively is an interest free loan until you pay it back at a silly rate, you could be better off. I am not saying abandon the government programs completely. I am saying don't rely on them and work with a financial advisor that can do these traditional program (as well as the age old program which we call Infinite Banking today).

This now brings me to the university circumstance I was speaking of earlier. University is a metaphor for an expense that props up and traumatizes parents during a time that should be joyful. The expense could be a wedding, family reunion or a dream vacation property. Typically your savings are in "prison". I call it such because you can't access them without getting hit tax-wise and you can't borrow against them. This is extremely problematic and has caused terrible financial stress for families and businesses I work with on a daily basis.

Infinite Banking makes all of these adversities an opportunity. Think in terms of the spend and grow rich with discipline theme. If you fund these lifetime milestones and dreams with your Infinite Banking system, not only are they tax free, you earn back the wedding or university expense, the same way you do with your car and vacation purchases. Discipline is the only catch. Nelson Nash's grocery store example on page 15 of "Becoming Your Own Banker" simply states the obvious: Discipline is needed in all businesses and ventures that are worthwhile and expected to be profitable.

RESP's are a great place to grow a nest egg for college or university. The myth, however, is that they are the best place to save for post-secondary education. The government grant for RESP's is 20% of annual deposits for up to a maximum annual contribution of $2500. The annual deposit plus the grant, totals $3,000 a year. As you can see below, at a 6% growth rate, these annual contributions grow to $98, 279 over eighteen years. This seems like a great plan, if you are not aware of the "Bank On Yourself" alternative.

Present Value (Money Paid):	**$0.00**
Future Value (Balance in Favor):	**$98,279.98**
Annual Payment (Money Paid):	**$3,000.00**

Period:	**18.00 yrs**
Annual Interest:	**6.000 %**

What made me ignore the benefits of becoming your own banker at first was the difference the grants make in the first 18 years. With the grants you have $ 98,000. Without the grants, you have approximately $ 82,000. If you stop there, the decision to make is clear. But children's lives don't stop there! The following spreadsheets will demonstrate how not interrupting the growth of your capital, makes the government grant look like a gimmick, if you think long term. Thinking long term is a must for financial security. See below:

Present Value (Money Paid):	**$0.00**
Future Value (Balance in Favor):	**$81,899.98**
Annual Payment (Money Paid):	**$2,500.00**
Period:	**18.00 yrs**
Annual Interest:	**6.000 %**

If you become the banker, and lend yourself the money and not interrupt the compounding growth of your savings, by age 40, your child's account has grown to $295,000. This example is no different than the problem paying cash for depreciable presents. When you pay cash for something, you lose the opportunity to ever earn money on that cash. Becoming your own banker prevents that enormous loss of capital growth.

Present Value (Money Paid):	**$81,899.00**
Future Value (Balance in Favor):	**$295,126.11**
Annual Payment (Money Paid):	**$0.00**
Period:	**22.00 yrs**
Annual Interest:	**6.000 %**

If you project out to the traditional retirement age of 65, you can see the awesome power of compound interest combined with the strategy of not interrupting your growth of capital. It's a seven-figure opportunity cost to your children!

Present Value (Money Paid):	**$81,899.00**
Future Value (Balance in Favor):	**$1,266,643.11**
Annual Payment (Money Paid):	**$0.00**
Period:	**47.00 yrs**
Annual Interest:	**6.000 %**

The dividend performance will obviously vary. In either case, not interupting the compounding growth of the capital makes an enoromous difference over time. This is the practice of not disrupting your ability to earn a return on your capital, whether you need it to fund purchases or not. On average, 90% or more of our capital is destroyed acquiring things traditionally (by using cash or credit). Infinite Banking solves this.

Chapter 11

INFINITE BANKING CANADA VS. USA

"If I have seen farther, it is only by standing on the shoulders of giants"
—Sir Isaac Newton

When I finally saw the financial "arrow" that Infinite Banking represents, I started devouring literature from the reformed advisors that have been practicing Infinite Banking for many years, if not decades. I read 28 books from mentors and authors such as Nelson Nash, Dan Thompson, Dr. Tom McVie, Barry Dyke, Pamela Yellen, Joe Kane, Mary Lyon, Ron Poteet, Joshua Thompson, Marc Burnel, Tom Langford, Kim Butler, George Antone and Bryan S. Bloom. It was a wonderful financial journey of awareness, with a glaring omission. All of these authors are American! They are writing to Americans and naturally, the one nagging question I had was: would this work as well for Canadians? Once I started mentally repackaging what I already knew, it made sense that there is no reason this can't work here. There are SOME differences, however. If you understand the makeup of a dividend paying whole life policy, you understand right away that this is and was the original tax free savings account without the government's promotion. Therefore, you can appreciate why governments would be wary of how much money was allowed to be put in these tax advantaged vehicles. All deposits, whether they are personal or coporate, are required to be made with after tax dollars, just like a Tax Free Savings Account. If you leave the money and dividends in the policy, your money compounds tax free for life. If you withdraw the dividend annually, they are tax free up until the adjusted cost base is reached. In non-financial jibberish, the adjusted cost base is the total contribution to the plan after withdrawals.

When my high net worth clients read how Infinite Banking works and how it improves every financial area of their lives, they want to pile the majority of their liquid savings in all at once It is THE savings vehicle and can be instantly deployed to acquire investments or major purchases of any kind, with no hassle or underwriting, all the while making five to seven times what their liquid savings account are earning them. It is no surprise I've never been busier!

Here's the challenge: to continue blessing this tax advantage program that has been around longer than the tax code. The government demands an insurable interest exists to justify the underwriting of the policy. This means that there has to be a justifiable financial loss that would result from the insured as a result of the insured's death. The funding of this policy has to be done in an annual, gradual fashion according to limits the government places on each insurance company. There is not an infinite capacity here. The government has already capped what each insurance company can allow their policy owners to tax shelter on an annual basis. For this reason, the capitalization of the policy (or Banking System, as I like to say) has to be done over a ten to twenty year period or longer if you choose. It can't be funded in one year to compensate the life insurance company for the lifetime of liability they take on for the death benefit. This death benefit, incidentally, becomes a bonus that makes it different for higher net worth individuals and their businesses. The premiums represent the present value of the death benefit. The monthly or annual deposit of premiums capitalizes the banking system and allows you to use the cash for you cash flow management; such as spend and grow rich, financing your own business or investments.

In the United States, policies can be funded and paid up in a shorter period of time than in Canada. This means that more money can be put into a policy in the US in the short term. This is very advantageous for both business and individual banking systems. I suspect this might change and their model will look more like Canada's, however this is my personal speculation.

In Canada, the amount you can deposit in a compliant way which satisfies the CCRA, is significantly less. However, it's not limited to the extent that you can't make it work for you. The limits are quite high. An average person can deposit over $15,000 a year. You might be required to do it for ten years, let's say, to satisfy the compliant tax advantaged illustration of the policy. In the US, you could do it in seven years or less which represents much more cash available up front to capitalize the banking or cash flow management system. For most people this is not an issue. For high net worth businesses, you need to work with an advisor that understands Infinite or Private Banking to make sure you won't be off the mark regarding tax compliance. Conversly, there are no minimums in both countries.

Another major difference between the US and Canada is the amount of choice one has regarding insurance companies that are still mutual. The importance of working with a mutual company is simple; you own the company as a policy owner and by default you are a holder as well. This gives you control over changes the company might want to make, which you would be eligible to vote for. You also are first in line for dividends without having to compete with shareholders that are in preferred position versus yourself. A stock company on the other hand, has already demutualized in the form of a public offering. Independent institutions and individual shareholders own the company. You technically don't own your own banking system, with a stock company. The concept still works with a stock company, if changes are not voted in which are against your wishes. The control, however, is not to the same extent, and for this reason the leading authority on Infinite Banking, Mr. Nelson Nash, does not recommend working with a stock company. He recommends a mutual company which fulfills the "Becoming Your Own Banker" mandate.

The United States also has many more choices regarding finding a mutual versus a stock company. In Canada, there is only one large mutual life insurance company which has not gone public yet: Equitable Life of Canada. There are others and I can use all of them, however for obvious reasons, I need to work with a strong one. It will be quite lucrative for policy holders when Equitable Life eventually chooses to become a stock company. Dividend paying life policy holders whose company went public in the last round of demutualizations got paid quite handsomely to have their voting rights taken away. The companies went public at book values. That alone is not a reason to do this. It could happen next year or thirty years from now.

A question I often get regarding this program is this: Alberto, this program is great, what if the government changes the rules? My answer is this: anything is possible with government. The factual reality tells the story best. To stay tax compliant, and have tax free benefits when they pay out, these policies need to be paid for with after tax dollars. The second, is that the amounts deposited have to follow the tax compliant illustrations of a life insurance company. I like to talk about these illustrations as banking systems, however at the root of the system are the principles of tax advantaged dividend paying life insurance. These dividend paying policies can only accept deposits that honour the present value calculations. If the government took away these principles, how well are they representing the voters in regards to their collective estate planning objectives? Not at all. In fact, if you look at how legislation is set up now, I would argue they have already reacted in a fashion that Canadians are concerned about. I know this because I have numerous clients (myself included) that wanted to deposit a lot more than the government would allow the insurance companies to illustrate and take on as deposits. The rules are very tight already and tax avoidance is not the overriding principle here. It is superior cash flow management with extremely positive estate planning benefits that are an acquired bonus with minimal cost, if you think long term. Remember, this system has been around for over 150 years and it pre dates the tax code. It is a legal contract that acts as a living trust.

In life, anything is possible. If you do nothing, you definitely lose. I have demonstrated the dangers of relying on programs like RRSP's exclusively for financial independence. I don't recommend relying on one single plan to achieve financial independence. I recommend multiple streams of income to achieve financial independance. I believe that Infinite Banking must be one of those multiple streams of income; perhaps the dominant one. If you are interested in guaranteed income for life, it should be the core of that stream of income that provides this guaranteed income for life. Infinite Banking works into a well integrated financial plan that takes all asset classes into account, not just two or three that are emphasized in Canadian banks or traditional brokerages that are extended branches of the Pirates of Manhattan.

Chapter 12

THIS IS FOR YOU!

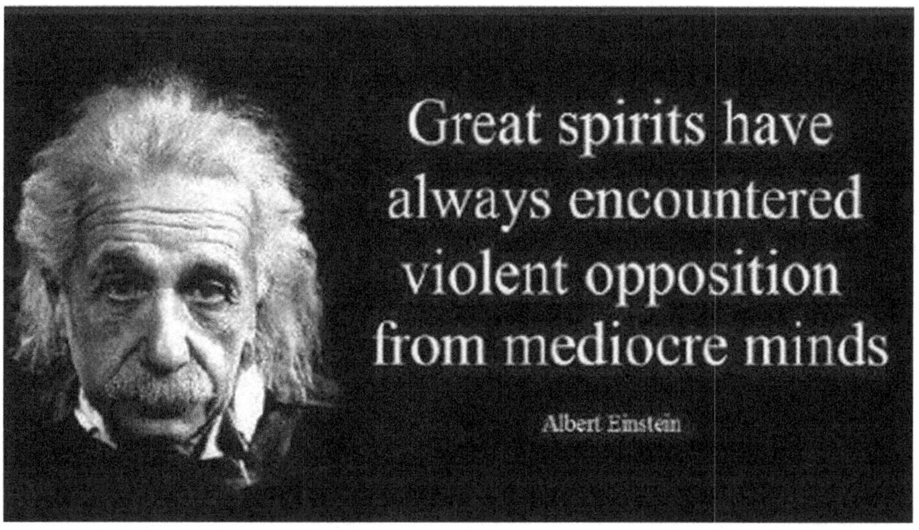

I have been very critical of the financial services industry. I have also been very honest that I was part of the problem due to the manufactured consent on what the "right" financial solutions are for individuals and corporations. The majority of the individuals in the financial services industry are well-intentioned individuals who are doing their best to add value to the lives of the people they are trying to help. What is disappointing, is the lack of holistic financial planning knowledge that integrates the risk management side with the wealth management side. I find you will have one point of view from the insurance professionals and a completely different one from the non-guaranteed world involving the financial markets. Fragmentation and special interest has caused our industry to lose its way. I have deliberately positioned myself to be able to speak knowledgeably about the valuable attributes of all four pillars of the financial planning spectrum. These pillars are Banking, Insurance, the Financial Markets and the Exempt Market (private security market). The financial individuals that can speak knowledgeably about all these four pillars are few and far between. Too often I see people who call themselves financial advisors and they have little or no knowledge of any of the other three sectors of the financial planning industry besides the one they are proficient with. This is where the consumer needs to be cognizant of whom they are working with.

There are few industries that are as competitive and outright stressful as the financial services industry. There are also few industries that can be as fulfilling. Helping someone achieve their dream of getting into their first home or protecting against financial adversity is extremely rewarding!

I went on a ten month journey to try and prove Nelson Nash, Pamella Yellen and Dan Thompson wrong. In the end, every objection I had was refuted with self-verified facts which reinforced why this strategy was a must for me, my clientele, my prospective clientele and every corporation that has positive cash flow in its operations. At the end of this journey, the reality was evident and the manufactured consent that I was a victim of had melted away.

Remember, the biggest purchasers of these dividend paying life policies are banks! The best book detailing that is called 'The Pirates of Manhattan' by Barry Dyke. The average person can add over a million dollars to their balance sheet by simply changing how they acquire their everyday necessities and luxuries. This is not exclusively for the financially wealthy or sophisticated. In fact, just as much value proportionately can be added to the average Joe's net worth as to a large corporate conglomerate.

I was part of the problem and now I am focused on a life long crusade to teach everyone I can how to reverse the financial slavery we have been forced to accept. If you had a cure for cancer, I am sure you would see it as your duty to tell the world! I have a cure for financial cancer.

Infinite Banking is a cure for the four financial cancers which plague every one! To review, these cancers are: paying interest to other entities besides yourself, inflation, taxes and depreciation on the items you consume and purchase every day. Infinite Banking gradually cures all of them. It is not get rich quick! It is save, spend, borrow from yourself and pay yourself back, with as high an interest rate you can that can grow tax free. We can become financially independent with a system that is infinite and replenishes itself. The financial planning systems we have been taught to embrace are finite and require you to continue feeding that system or have that system be subject to taxation that will greatly reduce the legacy to your family. The Infinite Banking system replenishes itself and legally creates a tax free legacy thanks to the benefits that have been inherent in dividend paying life insurance policies for over 150 years. This is an age-old approach that has been revitalized thanks to GIANTS such as Nelson Nash, Pamella Yellen, Dan Thompson, Dr.Tom McVie and Kim D.H. Butler. Like Isaac Newton famously said, "I am standing on the shoulders of Giants"

The credit goes to these people and I will do my best to honour their legacy and teach this system to as many people as my health will allow. This is not work for me. It is a fulfilling passion that I will never get tired of!

To review, what do you think builds more wealth? Taking risks and getting a "better return" on the ten percent you hope to save, or decreasing the total cost of building wealth by ending the acceptance or manufactured consent of losing 90% or more of your income and financial potential to taxes, interest, consumption and inflation? I hope I have demonstrated that the latter is a better strategy on a risk versus reward level and an absolute level not only adjusted for risk.

I am often asked why everyone isn't doing this. The reality is that everyone who understands Infinite Banking is doing it. Those that have read and seriously absorbed the principles of Infinite Banking possess uncommon knowledge. The majority of the people I have shared this material with have said they wish they had started this system many years ago. I can relate. I felt the exact same way. What gets me past this regret is the famous Chinese Proverb: "the best time to plant a tree was twenty years ago. The second best time is now".

RECOMMENDED READING

Prescription For Wealth- Dr. Tomas McFie
Becoming Your Own Banker – Nelson Nash
Warehouse Of Wealth – Nelson Nash
The Banker's Code – George Antone
Confessions of a CPA - Bryan S. Bloom
Bank On Yourself – Pamela Yellen
The Secret Asset - David D'Arcangelo
Safe Money Millionaire – Brett Kitchen
Killing Sacred Cows - Garrett Gunderson
The Pirates of Manhattan - Barry Dyke
The Creature From Jekyll Island - G. Edward Griffin
How Privatized Banking Really Works - L. Carlos Lara, Robert P. Murphy
Life Your Life Insurance – Kim D. H. Butler
Busting The Financial Planning Lies – Kim D. H. Butler
The Banking Effect– Dan Thompson
Discover Hidden Treasures – Dan Thompson
Bank on Yourself Revolution—Pamela Yellen
The Great Wall Street Retirement Scam—Rick Bueter
Simple Banking System—Joshua Thompson
The Power of Zero—David McKnight
Flash Boys—Michael Lewis
The Secret Asset—David D'Arcangelo
Money, Wealth, Life Insurance—Jake Thompson

Made in the USA
Middletown, DE
13 September 2019